As I open this book,
I open myself
to God's presence
in my life.

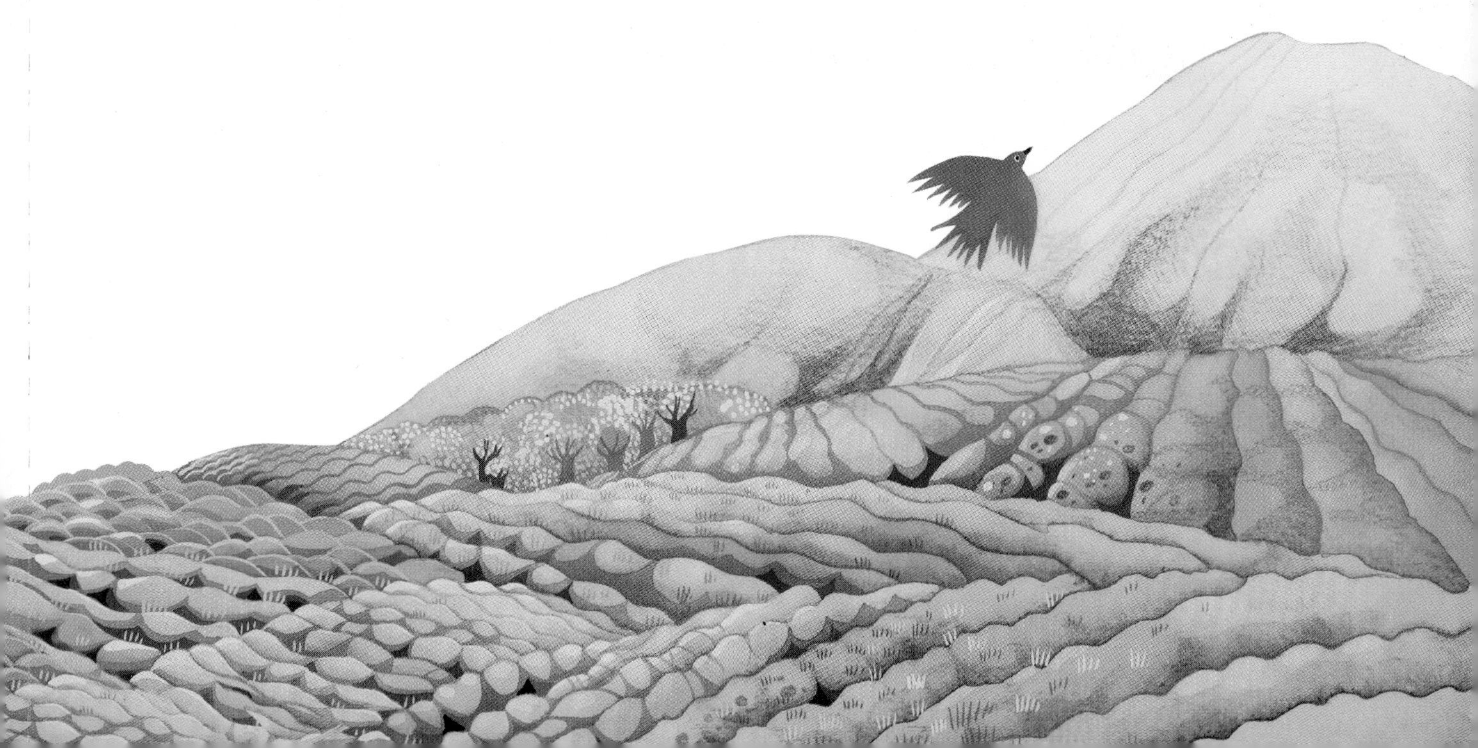

God's Invitation

*God calls me
to be aware of him
in all the people I know,
the places I go,
and the things I do each day.*

My Response

When I quiet myself to allow
God's grace to help me,
I see with truth,
hear with forgiveness,
and act with kindness
as God's love works through me.

Thank you God,
for your presence
in my life.

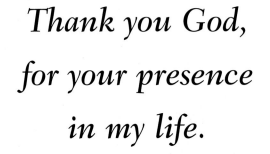

Finding God

Our response to God's gifts
3

Parish Edition

Barbara F. Campbell, M.Div., D.Min.

James P. Campbell, M.A., D.Min.

LOYOLAPRESS.

CHICAGO

Nihil Obstat Reverend John G. Lodge, S.S.L., S.T.D. Censor Deputatus August 20, 2003	**Imprimatur** Most Reverend Edwin M. Conway, D.D. Vicar General Archdiocese of Chicago August 22, 2003	The Ad Hoc Committee to Oversee the Use of the Catechism, United States Conference of Catholic Bishops, has found this catechetical text, copyright 2005, to be in conformity with the *Catechism of the Catholic Church.*

The *Nihil Obstat* and *Imprimatur* are official declarations that a book is free of doctrinal and moral error. No implication is contained therein that those who have granted the *Nihil Obstat* and *Imprimatur* agree with the content, opinions, or statements expressed. Nor do they assume any legal responsibility associated with publication.

Finding God: Our Response to God's Gifts **is an expression of the work of Loyola Press, an apostolate of the Chicago Province of the Society of Jesus.**

Senior Consultants
Jane Regan, Ph.D.
Richard Hauser, S.J., Ph.D., S.T.L.
Robert Fabing, S.J., D.Min.

Advisors
Most Reverend Gordon D. Bennett, S.J., D.D.
George A. Aschenbrenner, S.J., S.T.L.
Paul H. Colloton, O.P., Ph.D.
Eugene LaVerdiere, S.S.S., Ph.D., S.T.L.

Peg Bowman, M.A.
Gerald Darring, M.A.
Brian DuSell, D.M.A.
Teresa DuSell, M.M.
Bryan T. Froehle, Ph.D.

Thomas J. McGrath
Joanne Paprocki, M.A.
Daniel L. Snyder, M.Div., Ph.D.
Christopher R. Weickert
Elaine M. Weickert

Catechetical Staff
Daniel W. Gast, M.A.
Jeanette L. Graham, M.A.
Marlene Halpin, O.P., Ph.D.
Thomas McLaughlin, M.A.
Joseph Paprocki, M.A.

Grateful acknowledgment is given to authors, publishers, photographers, museums, and agents for permission to reprint the following copyrighted material; music credits where appropriate can be found at the bottom of each individual song. Every effort has been made to determine copyright owners. In the case of any omissions, the publisher will be pleased to make suitable acknowledgments in future editions. Continued on page 311.

Cover Design: Think Design Group
Cover Illustrator: Christina Balit
Interior Design: Three Communication Design

LOYOLAPRESS.
3441 N. ASHLAND AVENUE
CHICAGO, ILLINOIS 60657
(800) 621-1008
www.LoyolaPress.org
www.FindingGod.org

06 07 08 09 10 11 12 13 Banta 10 9 8 7 6 5 4 3 2

Table of Contents

Creator and Father

AD DEI
MAJO- GLO-
REM RIAM

Saint Ignatius of Loyola

Saint Ignatius of Loyola recognized God in every living creature in the heavens and on earth. He saw God in plants, in animals, and especially in people.

Saint Ignatius of Loyola

Saint Ignatius of Loyola was born in Spain in 1491. He grew up in a noble family in the castle of Loyola. He was a soldier until he was wounded in a battle. He went home to get well. There he read about the lives of Jesus and the saints. He wanted to become a saint too.

Ignatius traveled to a monastery in Spain at Montserrat. There he saw the mountain and many of God's wonderful creatures. He prayed at the shrine of Our Lady of Montserrat. He laid down his sword and pledged his life to God. He gave away his fine clothes and dressed as a poor man.

Later Ignatius wrote down what he learned about God and Jesus. His book is called the *Spiritual Exercises*. He wrote it to help people grow closer to God. He tells us that God cares for all the things he created. If we want to know God, we begin by caring for the world God gives us. Ignatius's feast day is July 31.

Created to Be Happy

All of God's creation is good. He wants us to enjoy and care for it.
What do you see here that God made for us to enjoy and love?

PRAYER

*Jesus, my friend, help me grow closer to God while I care
for the things in my world.*

Small Wonders

Lorena and her friend Katie walked slowly through a park. They were looking for colorful leaves for a school project.

Lorena picked up a leaf. She knew she had found something special. The colors of the little leaf were so pretty and bright that it made her think about God. She thought how wonderful God must be to give this tiny leaf such beauty.

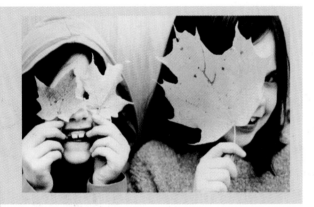

Lorena thought of how leaves change color and fall from the trees. She knew God would give the trees new green leaves in the spring. She thanked God in her heart for the beauty in her world.

Color this leaf to look like a beautiful fall leaf.

All Creation Praises God

Let all God's creation praise him, from the animals in the sea to the clouds in the sky. Mountains and trees, birds and animals praise God their creator. People young and old sing praise to God. His name alone is greater than heaven and earth.

adapted from Psalm 148:7-14

A Song of Praise

We have a feeling of wonder like Lorena had when we see the things God made for us. We tell God that we believe in him and love him. We sing praise to God.

Make your own song of praise. On the lines below, write a message to praise God for something beautiful you saw this week.

I love god for his kindness and me living and having life on earth I love the snow when it snows and I thank god for that!

We Believe in God

When we praise God, we show that we believe in him. We depend on him. We know that God blesses us and cares for us.

We pray a special prayer called the **Apostles' Creed** to show our faith. An **apostle** was a special follower of Jesus. A **creed** tells what people believe. The Apostles' Creed tells us what the apostles believed. It states the beliefs of our Catholic faith. This is how the Apostles' Creed begins. Learn this part and pray it often.

I believe in God, the Father almighty,
creator of heaven and earth.

Reading God's Word

God looked at everything he had made, and he found it very good.

Genesis 1:31

Knowing God

The beauty of the world helps us to know God. We see that God created all things because of his love. Because he created us and loves us, we make God important in our lives. We can know about God and creation by reading the Bible, which is the Word of God.

Loving God's Creation

We can love all of God's creation. Think of three people, animals, or parts of nature that you love. Draw pictures of them in the hearts. Write their names on the lines.

I love . . .

_____

_____

_____

PRAYER

I believe in God, the Father almighty,
creator of heaven and earth.

These are the first words of the Apostles' Creed, our very special faith prayer. Pray these words often.

Knowing that God is in your heart, think about him as Father of Jesus and your Father too. Then think about God making everything in the universe. Tell God how awesome he is! Thank him for his gift of creation. Tell God how you will keep our world beautiful.

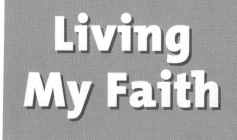

Living My Faith

Faith Summary

We believe in God, our Father, who created the world out of love for us. God wants us to know him and love him through the beauty of our world, which leads us to him.

Words I Learned

apostle   **Apostles' Creed**   **creed**

Ways of Being Like Jesus

You can be like Jesus when you love and care for all God's people and respect his creation.

With My Family

Respect your family and help them care for the world. Work together as a family to keep your neighborhood neat. Help take care of pets. Take care to recycle materials.

 PRAYER

Jesus, thank you for helping me to know and love God. Help me to care for God's world as he cares for me.

My Response

What will you do this week to show you care? Will you pick up litter? Will you encourage your friends to use the recycle bin? Draw a picture of what you will do to care for God's world.

a parent page

Focus on Faith

In Safe Hands With God

An old spiritual tells us "He's got the whole world in his hands." It is a vivid personal image of God, one that we are not always used to seeing. Many images of God show him looking at us from a distance. We can even be tempted to think that he is absent from the world. But God's care for us is always with us. It is ongoing and personal. Our gentle care for our children is like the gentle care of God. Our children may be concerned about what is happening in the world and wondering what will happen in the future. In the caring environment that we create, we can help give the assurance of God's gentle care and concern. The gentle care that our children experience through us today will help prepare them for recognizing God's presence in the future.

Hints for at Home

God teaches us through the Bible, which is his Word. Look at your family Bible or a children's Bible with your child. In this session your child read Genesis 1:31. The ideas for praising God in this session were based on Psalm 148:7–14. These verses are good choices for reading together.

Dinnertime Conversation Starter

Discuss favorite things you do together as a family and ways you show your love for one another.

Spirituality in Action

Emphasize to your child the importance of caring for our world. Separate items at home for recycling and encourage your child to recycle. You might explain that sharing clothes and games with younger brothers and sisters by "handing them down" is one kind of recycling. With your child, go through clothes and toys. Place unused or outgrown items that are in good condition in a "sharing bag" for a homeless shelter.

Focus on Prayer

The Apostles' Creed is our special faith prayer. Your child has learned the first sentence of the Creed. Help your child to practice praying this sentence. The complete Apostles' Creed can be found at www.FindingGod.org.

Your child also has reflected on the wonders of God's creation and about how to care for the things in our world. Spend some quiet time with your child thinking about the beauty in nature, or take a nature walk together. Share your thoughts, if you wish, or talk with Jesus silently.

Created to Be Together

God shares his love with us. He wants us to share his love with others. How can we help someone in need?

PRAYER

Jesus, show me how to help those in need so I can share your love for me, in the name of the Father, and of the Son, and of the Holy Spirit.

The Sign of the Cross

Each night before bed, Katie prayed the Sign of the Cross as she began her evening prayers. Julia copied her older sister, but she did not understand what she was doing.

"Why do we make that sign when we pray?" Julia asked.

Katie explained that the Sign of the Cross reminds us of the Trinity. We pray to the Father, the Son, and the Holy Spirit.

We pray to God our Father. He created all things because he loves us. We pray to the Son, Jesus. Jesus, the Son of God who became man, came to tell us of the Father's love and to save us. We pray to the Holy Spirit. The Holy Spirit helps us to understand how much God loves us. The Spirit helps us show God's love to others.

Link to Liturgy

Near the beginning of Mass we pray the Sign of the Cross. The same sign concludes the Mass.

Another Prayer to the Trinity

Katie told Julia of another prayer that praises God as the Trinity. She said, "When we pray the Glory Be to the Father, we are praising God, who created us. He is with us now and he always will be." Katie helped her sister pray this prayer.

Glory be to the Father, and to the Son, and to the Holy Spirit.
As it was in the beginning, is now, and ever shall be, world
without end.
Amen.

As they closed their prayer with the Sign of the Cross, Julia smiled. From now on, when she prays these prayers, she will think of the Trinity: the Father, the Son, and the Holy Spirit.

Reading God's Word

We have come to know and to believe in the love God has for us. God is love, and whoever remains in love remains in God and God in him.

1 John 4:16

Sharing God's Love

All love comes from God. God loves us so much that he sent his Son, Jesus, to give us life. We bring God's love to life in our world by loving one another.

adapted from 1 John 4:7-11

Showing Your Love

In the space below, write one way that you could show your love for a friend by helping him or her.

_____

_____

 Meet a Saint

Though her family was wealthy, Saint Elizabeth of Hungary lived a simple life. She devoted her life to feeding and clothing those who were poor. She started a hospital and cared for sick people. Elizabeth pleased God by sharing his love and being kind to those in need.

St. Elizabeth Clothes the Poor and Tends the Sick, **Anonymous**

Gentle Jesus

Jesus showed us how to love others. He used gentle words when he talked to people. Read the sentences below. Make a smiling face in the circle before each sentence that Jesus would like to hear you say. Make a frowning face in the circle next to the unkind sentences. Talk about what Jesus would say instead.

◯ Do you want to play with me?

◯ You cannot have any of my candy.

◯ You can go first.

◯ Do you want to come to my house?

◯ I do not like you.

◯ Let's ask Tommy to play.

◯ You cannot join my team.

PRAYER

In the name of the Father, and of the Son, and of the Holy Spirit. Amen. Let this be our prayer today. Think about the meaning of the words as we pray them again.

In the name of the Father,

Bring to mind some of the wonderful things God the Father has created.

and of the Son,

Imagine that you are walking with Jesus. What is Jesus telling you about God?

and of the Holy Spirit.

Think about the kind and caring things you do for others. The Holy Spirit helps you do these things.

Amen.

Spend a few more minutes with Jesus. Tell him how you will follow the guidance of the Holy Spirit. Tell him something you will do for another person. Thank him for his love.

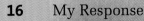

Faith Summary

The love of the Trinity—Father, Son, and Holy Spirit—is the source of our love. God wants us to share his love with others.

Ways of Being Like Jesus

Jesus helped people when they were sick or in need. You can be like Jesus by treating people kindly. You can offer to help others, even when you are busy.

With My Family

Cheerfully take your turn with family chores. Talk with your family about a neighbor for whom you could do a favor.

PRAYER

Jesus, thank you for showing me how to help others. Let me care for others like you did so I can grow closer to you.

My Response

What will you do this week to show your love for someone else? Write a sentence.

_____

_____

_____

Focus on Faith

The Sign of Blessing

A simple way that we identify ourselves as Christians is by praying the Sign of the Cross. We open and close our personal prayer time with the Sign of the Cross, but we can use it especially as a sign of blessing for our children. This simple gesture speaks of a very deep bond that we have with our children, deeper even than our human relationship with them. In praying the Sign of the Cross over them or on their foreheads, we acknowledge that God is the source of all of the blessings that our children receive through us. We acknowledge the limits of what we can do and open ourselves to the limitless source of God's love for us. Love is the gift we have received in our children and the gift we return in blessing.

Dinnertime Conversation Starter

S hare with your child a memory of a time when you realized that God had blessed you.

Spirituality in Action

Notice when your child does something special for someone else. Encourage him or her to continue being a willing helper. Do something as a family to help those less fortunate. This might be making a food basket for a family in need, shopping for a wish-tree gift at Christmas, or helping a sick or elderly neighbor with chores around the house.

Our Catholic Heritage

Since it started in 1975, Operation Rice Bowl has been contributing to Catholic Relief Services development projects. Thousands of parishes and schools participate in the program. Most of the contributions go to Catholic Relief Services to help people in 40 countries around the world. About 25 percent of the money donated stays in the local diocese. This emphasizes the importance of our responsibility to help our neighbors as well as people in need throughout the world. Visit **www.catholicrelief.org** for more information.

Focus on Prayer

The Sign of the Cross and the Glory Be to the Father bring to mind the Trinity. Your child has reviewed these prayers. Help your child practice praying them, using both words and gestures. Be sure that your child is aware of the Sign of the Cross at Mass.

God Is Our Father

As Jesus taught his disciples, they asked him many questions. What question would you have asked Jesus? Share your question if you like.

PRAYER

Jesus, my guide, teach me how to pray to God, our Father, so that I can grow in love for God and others.

Jesus Reveals God as Our Father

As God's Son, Jesus reveals to us what God is really like. He reveals that God is our Father, who cares for us as his children.

As God's children, we call God our Father, as Jesus did. *Father*, for Jesus, means the one who loves, forgives, and is good to his children. Sometimes Jesus called God **Abba**. That is a special name like Dad or Papa.

Children all over the world call God Father in their own language. The word for father in Spanish is *padre;* in German it is *Vater.* Do you know the word for father in another language?

Did You Know?

When we pray we raise our minds and hearts to God. We ask God for good things.

Jesus Teaches Us to Pray

Jesus went up the side of the mountain and sat down. His disciples gathered around him. Jesus began to teach them.

"This is how you are to pray:

Our Father, who art in heaven, hallowed be thy name; thy kingdom come; thy will be done on earth as it is in heaven. Give us this day our daily bread; and forgive us our trespasses as we forgive those who trespass against us; and lead us not into temptation, but deliver us from evil.

If you forgive others for the wrongs they do, your heavenly Father will forgive you."

adapted from Matthew 6:9-14

Caring Friends

You can be a caring friend to those who need you. You can do this by listening to people to understand how they feel. Unscramble these feeling words and tell how you would help someone who felt that way.

1. dsa   _sad_
2. argyn   _angery_
3. leolny   _lonley_
4. arafdi   _afraid_
5. kisc   _sick_
6. ghunry   _hungry_

Reading God's Word

Blessed be the God and Father of our Lord Jesus Christ. God the Father always shows us mercy. He encourages us. He supports us when we are troubled. He wants us to do the same for others who are suffering.

adapted from 2 Corinthians 1:3-4

As We Forgive Others

God wants us to care for others by thinking of their feelings.
He wants us to forgive others just as he forgives us.

What Would You Do?

Sometimes people do things that hurt us. Circle how you could
show forgiveness in these situations:

1. **Your little brother rode your new bike and fell. The chain came off.**

   A. You tell him he can never ride your bike again.

   B. You ask him if he is hurt and suggest you fix the bike together.

2. **Your good friend went to the park with another friend and did not invite you. Later she told you she was sorry she did not include you.**

   A. You tell her it is OK and invite both of them to play.

   B. You tell her you are not her friend anymore.

PRAYER

Jesus taught us the Lord's Prayer. He wanted to bring us closer to God the Father, to himself, and to one another. God is our loving Father, and we say our prayer to him.

> *Our Father, who art in heaven, hallowed be thy name; thy kingdom come; thy will be done on earth as it is in heaven.*

We give glory to God, whose name is holy. We pray that what he wants for us and for the world will happen.

> *Give us this day our daily bread; and forgive us our trespasses as we forgive those who trespass against us; and lead us not into temptation, but deliver us from evil. Amen.*

We ask God for what we need to live. We tell him we will forgive others as he forgives us. We ask him to keep us from evil.

Imagine that you are with Jesus and his disciples on the mountain. You have a chance to talk to Jesus alone. Tell Jesus what is the most important part of the prayer for you right now. Talk with him about it. Listen in your heart for what he wants you to know.

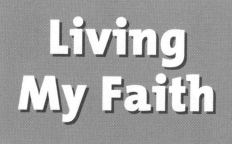

Living My Faith

Faith Summary

By teaching us the Lord's Prayer, Jesus reveals God as our Father. He tells us God wants us to live in peace with one another.

Word I Learned

Abba

Ways of Being Like Jesus

You can be like Jesus when you forgive others. Ask God to help you learn forgiveness from him.

With My Family

Live peacefully with your family. Show your love by helping family members without being asked.

PRAYER

Jesus, thank you for showing us how to pray to God, our Father. Help me forgive others so I can be more like you.

My Response

What will you do at home to show your love in a special way? Draw a picture of what you will do.

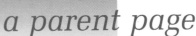

Focus on Faith

Jesus' Obedience and Ours

Obedience is a word that is easily misunderstood. We read that Jesus obeyed his Father. We wish that our children would be more prompt to obey. We can easily have the notion that obedience means automatic response to a command, but the root word for obedience means "to hear." An obedient person is one who listens with an understanding heart to what is being said. This is how Jesus listened to his Father. By being good listeners ourselves, we teach our children how to listen. Each of us is called as a parent to listen to our child so that we can hear what is in his or her heart. In this way we model Jesus' obedient response to his Father.

Dinnertime Conversation Starter

Share a story about a time when you felt that someone really listened to you. Talk about ways that you can all be better listeners.

Hints for at Home

Share family background and country-of-origin stories with your child. Help your child to understand that although we are different from one another, we are one human family with God as our Father. Have fun as a family learning words and phrases in different languages, such as those for father, mother, and God.

Spirituality in Action

Encourage your child to be open to understanding and helping all people, regardless of differences in background. Talk with your child about ways to help new students at school who may have difficulty with language or in making friends.

Focus on Prayer

Your child is reviewing the words and the meaning of the Lord's Prayer. Pray this special prayer with your child at home and as it is prayed or sung during Mass. You can find this prayer at www.FindingGod.org.

Jesus Is With Us

Mary and Joseph prepared for Jesus to be born. How do you think they got ready for Jesus? If you had been there, how would you have helped Mary and Joseph?

 PRAYER

Jesus, Savior, help me to learn from your life so that I can live as God wants me to.

Trusting in God

A young woman named Mary was engaged to a good man named Joseph. An angel visited Joseph in a dream and told him that Mary would have a baby through the Holy Spirit. The angel said the baby's name would be Jesus, which means "God saves us." Jesus was to be our Savior. Jesus would also have the name Emmanuel, which means "God is with us."

adapted from Matthew 1:18-23

Joseph listened to the angel and trusted in God. He and Mary got married. Jesus, the **Son of God,** was born. Joseph cared for Mary and Jesus.

Modern clay angel from Peru

Did You Know?

The name *Christ* means "the anointed one." That means the one chosen by God to be our Savior.

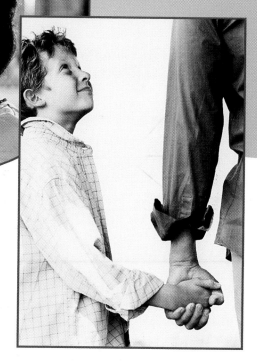

Listening and Trusting

In the **Scriptures** we learn that the angel visited Joseph in a dream. Joseph listened to the angel. He trusted in God and cared for Jesus and Mary.

Sometimes we must listen to others. We trust our parents and teachers when we do not know what to do. Can you think of a time when you listened and trusted what someone told you?

We trust in God. Jesus, God's Son who became man, is with us always. Even when we are alone or afraid, Jesus is with us.

Reading God's Word

The Lord leads you. He will always be with you. He will never disappoint you or abandon you. Do not be afraid or discouraged.

adapted from Deuteronomy 31:8

Names for Jesus

We have many special names for Jesus. These names tell us about Jesus. Draw lines to match each name with its meaning.

1. Emmanuel   the anointed one

2. Jesus   God is with us

3. Christ   God saves us

A Name Is Special

Jesus' followers had special names. Some names tell us something about the person. Peter's name means "rock." John's name means "God is gracious." Matthew's name means "gift of God."

Some names may have special meanings in your family. Do you know if your name has a special meaning? See if you can learn the meaning of your name.

Ramón
Origin: Spanish
Meaning: mighty protector

Nijeri
Origin: West African
Meaning: the warrior's daughter

Seamus
Origin: Irish
Meaning: may God protect him

Beth
Origin: Hebrew
Meaning: house of God

Examples for Living

Jesus showed us how to live the way God wants us to live. He spent his life teaching and healing others. Joseph also showed us ways of living a good life. He trusted in God and took care of Mary and Jesus.

Following an Example

People in our lives can show us good ways to live. Circle the pictures of the people below who set good examples for us.

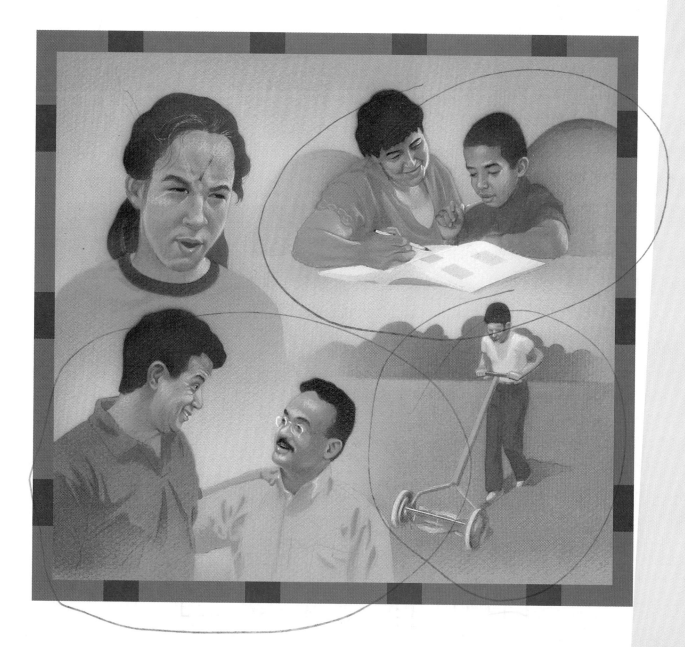

PRAYER

Joseph believed and trusted the angel who appeared to him. We tell God we believe in Jesus when we pray this part of the Apostles' Creed.

I believe in Jesus Christ, his only Son, our Lord.
He was conceived by the power of the Holy Spirit
and born of the Virgin Mary.

Pray this part of the Apostles' Creed in the presence of Jesus. Spend some time talking with him. Invite him to be at home in your heart just as he was at home with Joseph and Mary. Think about how you will make Jesus at home in your heart. Talk it over with him. Remember to say, "Thank you!"

St. Joseph and the Christ Child, Anonymous, painting on elk hide

Faith Summary

We believe that God sent his Son to save us and to be with us at all times. Through his own life Jesus reveals God's love for us and teaches us what it means to live as God wants us to live.

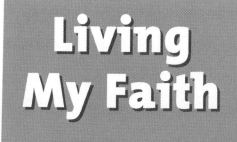

Living My Faith

Words I Learned

Scriptures   **Son of God**

Ways of Being Like Jesus

You can be like Jesus by following his example. He always helped others and was good to everyone. You can look for ways to help others.

With My Family

Jesus reached out to people who were hurting. Try to notice when someone in your family seems sad. Do something to make that person happy.

PRAYER

Jesus, thank you for always being with me. Help me to reach out to others and treat them kindly, as you did.

My Response

What will you do this week to help one person who seems unhappy? Draw a picture that shows how you will try to help him or her.

The Holy Family with Sparrow,
Bartolomeo Esteban Murillo

Focus on Faith

Joseph Was a Kind and Just Man

Joseph is not known as much for the job he had as for his relationship to his family. As the story in the Gospel of Matthew tells us, Joseph did not know what to make of Mary's situation until God revealed that she would be the mother of the Messiah. Joseph listened. He loved and cared. In response to Herod's threat, he led his family out of danger into an unknown land. He then led them home and protected them throughout his life. God is calling us as parents to lead our families into the future. He does not leave us alone in this task. The same Holy Spirit who led Mary and Joseph is here with us on the way in our journey of faith.

Hints for at Home

Help your child understand the importance of the family and the community as social institutions. You might play a simple game of "helping hands." Write out situations on cutout paper hands or on simple slips of paper. Have family members take turns choosing one situation and telling how they would help. Situations might include a neighbor who is sick, a child who is picked on, or a family that needs food.

Dinnertime Conversation Starter

Ask each person in the family to name something that he or she would like to ask Joseph about his life with Jesus and Mary. Discuss what his answers might be.

Spirituality in Action

Help your child to be sensitive to the feelings of others. Begin at home by discussing ways that family members speak to one another. Talk with your child about how curt, sarcastic, or mean words can hurt feelings. Discuss ways to avoid bullying with words at home and at school.

Focus on Prayer

In the Apostles' Creed we state our belief in Jesus, our Savior. Your child has been introduced to the first three sentences of the Creed. Help him or her to say and understand this part of the prayer. The remaining parts of the prayer will be learned in upcoming weeks. You can find this prayer at www.FindingGod.org.

Understanding Our Faith

Think about the words you have learned. Write each word on the line next to its meaning.

apostle	Trinity	praise	trespasses	Son of God
creed	Abba	God	Scriptures	Holy Spirit

1. _____ give glory to God

2. _____ sins against another

3. _____ name Jesus sometimes used for God

4. _____ what we believe

5. _____ follower of Jesus

6. _____ Father, Son, and Holy Spirit

7. _____ God's words to us in the Bible

8. _____ our Father

9. _____ Jesus Christ

10. _____ helps us to know God and love others

Hearts and Hands

We love with our hearts. We help with our hands. God wants us to share his love with others. We can be caring friends with our words and actions.

On each heart write something you will say to a family member or friend to show your love.

On each hand write something you will do to help someone in need.

Cut out the hearts and hands. Take them home as a reminder to say and do these things. You might paste the cutouts on a bow or ribbon for a wall decoration.

PRAYER SERVICE

Leader: Let us praise our loving God be God for ever.

All: Blessed be God for...

Leader: Let us pause to thank God the Father for his beautiful creation. We thank Jesus for revealing God to us. We thank the Holy Spirit for helping us to share God's love with the world.

All: Amen.

Reader: A reading from the first letter of John.

All love comes from God. God loves us so much that he sent his Son, Jesus, to give his life for us so our sins could be forgiven. We bring God's love to life in our world by loving one another.

[adapted from 1 John 4:7–11]

The Word of the Lord.

All: Thanks be to God.

Living My Faith

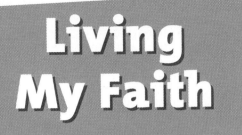

Ways of Being Like Jesus

You can be like Jesus by loving God and respecting our world. You can help and forgive others, even when it is hard to do.

With My Family

Talk with your family about taking care of our world. Keep your neighborhood clean. Help those who are not well enough to do things by themselves.

PRAYER

Jesus, my Savior, thank you for being with me at all times. Show me how to serve others as I try to follow your example.

My Response

Think of someone you do not know very well, but who needs help. Can you and your family help this person this week? Write a sentence to tell what you will do to help him or her.

_____

_____

Son of God, Son of Mary

Saint Scholastica and Saint Benedict

Saint Scholastica and her twin brother Saint Benedict lived in the hills of northern Italy. When they grew up, they each started a religious community.

Saint Scholastica and Saint Benedict

Saint Scholastica and her brother Saint Benedict grew up together in the hills of northern Italy. They were best friends. When they moved apart, they missed each other very much.

Benedict went to study in Rome. Scholastica stayed close to home. She loved to study and to take care of people who were poor or sick.

Later Scholastica started a community of nuns. It was about five miles from the monastery where Benedict had started a community of monks. Scholastica and Benedict met once a year in a little house nearby. They prayed and talked about their love of God.

At the end of one visit, Scholastica asked her brother to stay longer. When he refused, she prayed that he would stay. A powerful storm started and Benedict could not leave. Scholastica explained that since he would not listen to her, she had asked God. She said God had heard her prayer. They talked and prayed all night. Scholastica's feast day is February 10. Benedict's feast day is July 11.

Jesus' Good News

Many stories teach lessons about how to live.
Name a fairy tale or another story that teaches a lesson.

![prayer hands] **PRAYER**

*Jesus, my teacher, help me to understand your stories, so they can
help me to know and love God and others.*

The Kingdom of God

Many people gathered around to hear Jesus speak. Jesus wanted them to understand what the Kingdom of God is like. He told them this story, or parable.

"The Kingdom of God is like a mustard seed that is planted in a field. It is the smallest of all seeds, but it grows to be the largest of plants. It becomes a bush so large that birds come and nest in its branches."

adapted from Matthew 13:31-32

Jesus used this story to show how, with God's help, a great, welcoming kingdom can grow from small beginnings. Small acts of kindness can help many people feel welcomed by God.

Saint Benedict Serves the Kingdom

Benedict, twin brother of Scholastica, founded a **monastery** in Monte Cassino in Italy. This was the home for a group of men called monks who wanted to work and pray together.

Benedict wrote rules for how the monks should live. He taught the monks that they could praise God by daily work and prayer. They worked on the land, prayed, and copied the Bible by hand. Benedict's motto was "pray and work." Several of Benedict's rules are listed below.

Some monks left and started other monasteries. Saint Benedict's work was like planting a mustard seed. The small seed of his monastery sprouted many branches.

Seek Jesus' love above all else.

Do not speak evil of others.

Let a wise man stand at the gates of the monastery to greet visitors.

A brother's clothing should be suited to the weather where he lives.

? Did You Know?

The name *Benedict* means "blessed." A benediction is a blessing.

We Serve God's Kingdom

The Kingdom of God calls us to follow Jesus by loving one another and living according to God's rule and direction.

During his life in Nazareth, Jesus worked hard and observed the rules of the Jewish faith. He loved all people. Jesus showed that we can serve God's kingdom in our daily lives.

Here is an example of what Jesus meant. Anna, a third grader, goes to Mass with her family. One Sunday, the priest said there were children in the parish who needed hats and gloves for winter. Anna went home and returned with a pair of warm mittens. Her friend Tara saw her and did the same thing. Soon many others did too. Anna's small beginnings served God's kingdom.

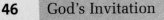

Can You Be Like Yeast?

When we make a loaf of bread, we add just a little yeast to make the dough rise. Yeast is like the mustard seed—a little bit makes a big difference.

Small things we do can be like yeast. By doing small things, we can serve God's kingdom. On the rising dough below, write one small thing you can do to serve the kingdom. On the bowl, write how this act helps the kingdom to grow.

_____

_____

_____

_____

Reading God's Word

Jesus told the people a parable about yeast. He said the Kingdom of God is like yeast that a woman mixes with wheat flour to make dough rise. Even though the amount of yeast is small, it can make the dough rise.

adapted from Matthew 13:33

PRAYER

Jesus' parables are like puzzles. When Jesus told them, people sometimes asked for help to understand them. Think about the parables of the mustard seed and the yeast.

Imagine that you are there when Jesus is telling one of these parables. Who is with you? Do people look puzzled as Jesus tells the story?

Do you understand what Jesus is saying about the Kingdom of God? How does the parable help you understand what he means?

Now spend some time with Jesus. Thank him for telling stories to help you understand God's direction in your life. Tell him one thing you will do to serve God's kingdom.

Faith Summary

Jesus' parables teach us that we can serve the Kingdom of God in our own lives. Jesus teaches us that small acts of kindness can make a big difference.

Word I Learned

monastery

Ways of Being Like Jesus

You serve the Kingdom of God when you do small things to help others. You can say something nice to a classmate and offer your help at home when it is needed.

With My Family

Ask a parent to bake some bread with you. Talk about the yeast parable with your family.

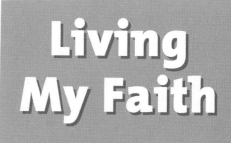

 PRAYER

Thank you, Jesus, for teaching me the importance of all the things that I do. Help me as I try to make a difference.

My Response

Think of a small project to help someone in need in your school, neighborhood, or parish. Encourage others to join you. Draw a picture of what you will do.

Focus on Faith

Beginning Small

Our children are fascinated with how and why things grow. Either in school or at home, they may at some time have taken a small seed, planted it, watered it, and, with patience, watched it grow. Perhaps the plant had to be transplanted into a larger pot or into the ground to give its roots room to spread. From the tiniest beginnings, flourishing plants grow. It is no surprise that when Jesus spoke to his people in an agricultural society, he used this image to describe the growth of the Kingdom of God. In the same way, relationships within families are built on small acts of kindness and consideration. These small acts provide the foundation every family needs to grow together when facing the stresses of daily life.

Dinnertime Conversation Starter

Discuss together what you can do this week for family time. You might share a bag of popcorn and a rental movie, play a board game, take a walk, or have ice cream cones. Plan a special time when the family can be together.

Hints for at Home

This is a good opportunity for the family to read the Bible together. You could read the mustard seed parable in Matthew 13:31–32, Mark 4:30–32, and Luke 13:18–19. Discuss the lesson that Jesus was teaching. Talk about how the wording of the parable may vary, but the message remains the same. Discuss how Jesus used simple stories to explain complex ideas.

Spirituality in Action

Encourage your child to keep in mind the small things that he or she can do to serve God's Kingdom. These may include being polite and friendly or helping friends or family members without being asked. Praise your child for doing small favors for others.

Focus on Prayer

Your child has read and talked about the parables of the mustard seed (Matthew 13:31–32) and the yeast (Matthew 13:33). Talk about these stories with your child. Help your child to understand that his or her commitment to love others serves the Kingdom of God.

Following Jesus

Have you ever followed someone when you didn't know which way to turn? When have you put your trust in another person?

PRAYER

Jesus, my guide, show me what is really important in life, so I can do what is important to you.

The Rich Young Man

One day a young man stopped Jesus. "Good teacher," he asked, "what must I do to gain eternal life?"

"You must keep the Ten Commandments," Jesus replied.

The young man smiled. "That is easy. I have kept the Commandments since I was a child," he said.

Christ and the Rich Young Ruler, Heinrich Hofmann

Jesus looked at the young man with love. "There is one more thing you should do," he said. "Sell everything you own and give the money to the poor. Then come, follow me."

The young man frowned. He went away, for he was very rich.

Jesus said to his disciples, "It is not easy for people with wealth to choose God's kingdom!"

adapted from Mark 10:17-23

What do you think the rich young man will do next?

Choosing God

God does not expect us to give up everything we have, but he does call us to change. He wants us to love him above all else. He wants us to love one another as much as we love ourselves.

God gave us the Ten Commandments to show us how to love him and one another. When we make wrong choices, we turn away from God and others. These choices lead us into sin. God calls us to be sorry for our sins. The Holy Spirit gives us the grace to turn back to God. We then mend our relationships with God and others. This is called **conversion.**

Every day we make choices about how to act toward God and others. The Ten Commandments help us to follow God and to care for others.

Link to Liturgy

When we follow the Ten Commandments, we live peacefully with one another. As we offer the sign of peace at Mass, we share the peace of Christ with one another.

Obeying the Ten Commandments

By obeying the Ten Commandments, we show respect to God and others and live our lives without harming anyone. Jesus teaches us that this is a good thing. But Jesus asked the rich young man to do more. He asked him to give up all that he owned and follow him. The rich young man was not willing to do this.

Taking the Next Step

We are sometimes called to give up things we want, but do not need. Draw an X through the things you may want, but do not need.

Did You Know?

The world is full of people in need. One of every seven people in the world does not get enough food to eat. Think of what you can do to help one person who doesn't get enough to eat.

Showing Our Love

The rich young man was not ready to change. Giving up his wealth was too hard. Sometimes it is hard for us to give up things and follow Jesus. Buying the newest video game can seem more important than helping others. Playing with friends can seem more important than cleaning up the neighborhood.

We can show our love for God and our neighbor by praying often, by keeping an open heart, and by always being ready to help.

 **Reading God's Word**

For where your treasure is, there also will your heart be.

Matthew 6:21

PRAYER

Imagine you are there when Jesus is talking to the rich young man. You see and hear everything. You see how sad Jesus is as he watches the young man walk away. If you could talk with the young man, what would you say?

After Jesus watches the young man leave, you and Jesus take a walk. When he looks at you, what do you tell him? What do you ask him? Walk quietly with Jesus, glad to be together.

Faith Summary

The Ten Commandments tell us how to love God and others. God gives us the grace to change and to cooperate with him.

Word I Learned

conversion

Ways of Being Like Jesus

You can be like Jesus when you do things for others cheerfully, even if it's not convenient. You can be generous to people who are in need.

With My Family

See if there is anything around your home that someone else could use, such as clothes or toys that are in good condition. Gather them in a box and donate them to a shelter or charity.

PRAYER

Thank you, Jesus, my friend, for showing me how to love you so much. I will follow you.

My Response

What could you do this week to show you want to follow Jesus? Write a sentence.

_____

_____

Focus on Faith

Jesus Asks Us to Dream

As parents, we do our best to take care of our children's basic needs. In the story of Jesus and the rich young man, we see that the young man has taken care of the basic needs in his life. He follows the Commandments and Jesus loves him. Then Jesus asks the young man to dream, to go beyond the basics, but the man walks away. Jesus is also asking us to dream. How can we as parents use our imaginations to discover ways to love our children that call us beyond giving them the basic things they need?

Dinnertime Conversation Starter

Talk about what you think it would be like to follow Jesus. How did he travel? What did he eat? Where did he sleep? What do you think life was like for a follower of Jesus? Would you like to travel with him, or would that be scary?

Christ and the Rich Young Ruler, Heinrich Hofmann

Our Catholic Heritage

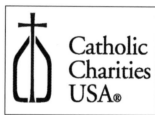

In 1910 a number of Catholic charities convened to create a group whose mission in part was to be the "attorney for the poor." The organization that later would be called Catholic Charities USA was born. Today, more than 1,400 agencies, institutions, and organizations make up the Catholic Charities network. Its mission is to provide high-quality services for people in need, to advocate justice in social structures, and to call the entire Church and other people of good will to do the same. Find out more about Catholic Charities USA at **www.catholiccharitiesusa.org**.

Spirituality in Action

If you contribute to a charity, involve your child when you make a donation. Explain what the charity does and how the contributions help. If you are not a regular contributor, you might talk with your child about a charity you could choose to help as a family. Talk with your child about the importance of giving up things we want in order to help those who do not have what they need.

Focus on Prayer

Your child has reflected on the story of the rich young man (Mark 10:17–23). Read the story together and spend a few quiet moments thinking about how you would answer Jesus' call.
You may share your thoughts with your child if you wish, but allow your child to choose whether or not to share his or hers with you.

Jesus Gathers Disciples

Think of a time you worked together with your friends to make something happen. What did you do?

 PRAYER

Loving Jesus, show me how to be your friend, so I can be a friend to others.

Jesus Calls Peter

The **Gospels** tell the good news of Jesus' life. In the Gospel of Luke, we learn how Jesus called Peter to follow him.

Jesus was near a lake, sharing the word of God with many people. He saw two boats with fishermen washing their nets. Jesus got into Peter's boat and asked him to move the boat away from the shore. Jesus taught the crowd from the boat.

Later he asked Peter to move the boat into deeper water and to lower the fishing nets. Peter answered, "We have worked all night long without catching anything. But if you tell me to, I will lower the nets."

adapted from Luke 5:1-5

Would you trust Jesus as Peter did?

Peter Answers the Call

Peter knew he could do more with Jesus' help than by himself. He trusted Jesus and lowered the nets into the water. The fishermen caught so many fish that their nets were tearing. They called to their partners on the other boat to come and help them.

Soon both boats were so full of fish that they almost sank. The fishermen were amazed. Peter knelt in front of Jesus and said, "Leave me, Lord, for I am a sinful man."

Jesus accepted Peter as he was. He called Peter to help him bring others to God. "Do not be afraid," Jesus said to him. "From now on you will be catching people instead of fish." When they reached the shore, Peter and the others left everything behind and followed Jesus.

adapted from Luke 5:6-11

Proclaiming the Kingdom

Jesus knew he needed help to spread God's word. He chose Peter and the other apostles and sent them out to preach. He also chose other followers called disciples to help with his work. Jesus' apostles and disciples accepted the **mission** that Jesus gave them to proclaim God's kingdom.

Jesus told Peter to use the talents God gave him to help bring others to God. What qualities do you think Jesus looked for in his apostles and disciples?

Did You Know?

Jesus chose 12 apostles to lead the Church. The pope and bishops of the Catholic Church continue the apostles' mission today.

Bishops gathered at Saint Peter's Basilica in 1962 for the Second Vatican Council.

Working Together to Follow Jesus

It often takes many people working together to do a job.
Jesus' apostles learned to work together when they went out
to proclaim God's word. Write how you could work with others
to follow Jesus' path.

_____

_____

_____

_____

_____

Reading God's Word

Jesus told his disciples to gather followers. He said they would be like
workers during a harvest. He said, "There is a large crop but few
workers. More workers are needed to bring in the crop."

adapted from Luke 10:2

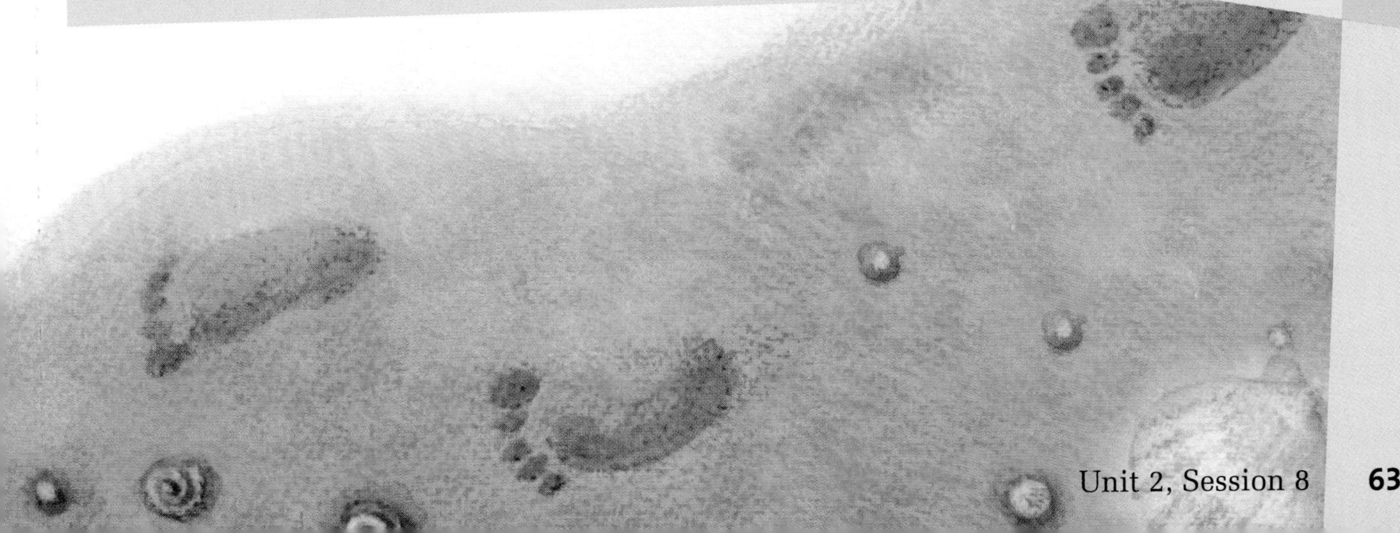

PRAYER

Imagine that you are standing with the people on the shore of the lake. The sun has just risen. What colors do you see in the sky? What else do you see? What are some of the smells along the shore? Listen as Jesus talks to the people from the boat. What might he be saying?

Imagine that it is a little later and the boats are back at shore. Watch Peter and the others leave everything and follow Jesus.

Imagine that Jesus, Peter, and the others walk toward you as they are leaving. Picture yourself walking through the sand in your bare feet to meet Jesus. Jesus is calling you. What is your answer?

Spend a few minutes with Jesus. Tell him you want to be his friend. Tell him what you will do to follow him.

Faith Summary

Jesus chose apostles and sent them on a mission to preach the word of God. He also chose disciples to help him. Jesus wants us to proclaim the Kingdom of God.

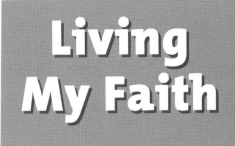

Words I Learned

Gospel   **mission**

Ways of Being Like Jesus

You are like Jesus when you work well with others. When you work in a group, listen to others and respect their ideas.

With My Family

Think of someone you know who is sick. How could you cheer up that person? You could draw a picture, write a letter, or make a visit to brighten his or her day.

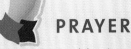 **PRAYER**

Dear Jesus, like Peter I trust you to guide my life. Thank you for calling me to follow you.

My Response

Draw a picture of your family working together on a project you think might be helpful to someone in need.

Focus on Faith

Jesus Sees Possibilities

When Jesus called Peter to be his disciple, Peter asked him to leave. Peter did not see the possibilities that Jesus did. Peter was an intelligent man with an established trade. He did not want to think beyond day-to-day concerns, but Jesus recognized Peter's talents and called him to become the leader of the Church. As parents we have the best opportunity to recognize and nurture the talents of our children. Many parents are tempted to see in a child possibilities that do not suit the child's personality or abilities. By recognizing and nurturing each child's true talents and abilities, we can help our children become who God is calling them to be.

Dinnertime Conversation Starter

Tell your children some of your dreams. Ask them, "What do you want to be when you grow up? Why?" Listen to their dreams and encourage the development of their talents.

Spirituality in Action

Jesus called Peter personally. The need to be connected is as strong as the need for food. As a family, make a list of people who would like to hear from you or with whom you haven't gotten in touch for a while. Phone, send an e-mail message, or write to them.

Focus on Prayer

Your child has read and reflected on the Gospel story of Jesus calling Peter (Luke 5:1–11). Help your child to understand that he or she receives a personal call from Jesus to be his special friend and follower. Encourage your child to spend a few quiet moments thinking about accepting Jesus' call as Peter did.

Our Catholic Heritage

The Society of St. Vincent de Paul was started in Paris, France, in 1833 by a group of students who were challenged to show the good works of the Catholic Church. The society was formed to minister to the needs of poor people. The society spread to the United States in 1845. Today this international group gives people of all backgrounds a chance to serve those in need. An example of the virtue of solidarity in action, the society provides many services, including assisting elderly men and women, helping people with disabilities to find jobs, and operating thrift stores, nurseries, shelters, and rehabilitation facilities.

Vincent and the Beggar, Meltem Aktas

Jesus Dies and Rises

Think of ways you can share God's love by caring for the people, animals, and other living things around you. What can you do?

PRAYER

Jesus, my Savior, give me the grace to serve others as you did, so that I can live the faithful life God wants me to live.

Remember My Message

Saint Paul wrote a letter to his friends in Corinth. He was worried that they had forgotten what he had told them about Jesus' death and resurrection. This is what Paul wrote so that the people in Corinth would believe and be saved.

Saint Paul (detail), Anonymous, the Getty Epistles

Friends,
Remember the gospel I preached to you. If you believe this message, you will be saved.

Jesus Christ died for our sins, as the Scriptures say. He was buried. He was raised from the dead three days later. He appeared to Peter and the apostles.

adapted from 1 Corinthians 15:1-5

We Proclaim Jesus' Death and Resurrection

After he died, Jesus opened the gates of heaven for the just people who had died before him. Then he rose from the dead and appeared to Peter and the apostles. We call Jesus' passage from death to resurrection the **Paschal Mystery.**

Because Jesus Christ is God, we call him Lord. He was raised by the Father through the power of the Holy Spirit. Jesus Christ shares his life with us by sending the Holy Spirit to us. From the Holy Spirit, we receive the grace to be faithful to God and serve others. If we do this, we will be with Jesus at the end of time.

The Holy Resurrection, Nana Quparadze

Reading God's Word

Jesus said, "I am the resurrection and the life. Everyone who lives and believes in me will never die."

adapted from John 11:25-26

Resurrection, Solomon Raj

We Believe

In this part of the Apostles' Creed, we proclaim our belief in the Paschal Mystery. Pray this part of the creed.

He suffered under Pontius Pilate,
    was crucified, died, and was buried.
He descended to the dead.
On the third day he arose again.
He ascended into heaven,
    and is seated at the right hand
        of the Father.
He will come again to judge the living
    and the dead.

Link to Liturgy

We celebrate the Paschal Mystery at Mass when we pray, "Christ has died, Christ is risen, Christ will come again."

Celebrating New Life

Liliana and Amy peeked excitedly into their butterfly box. They had seen the eggs hatch into caterpillars. The caterpillars ate so many leaves that they outgrew their skins several times. Then the caterpillars spun silky cocoons around themselves. The cocoons rested quietly for two weeks.

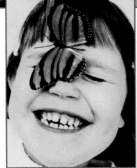

At last, the cocoons seemed ready to burst. The girls wondered if this would be the day the former caterpillars would fly off and start their new lives as butterflies.

Liliana told Amy that she learned in church that the butterfly is a symbol of Jesus' resurrection. When the butterfly comes out of the cocoon, we are reminded of Jesus' resurrection.

Color the Butterfly

Color this butterfly, ready to fly off to a new life.

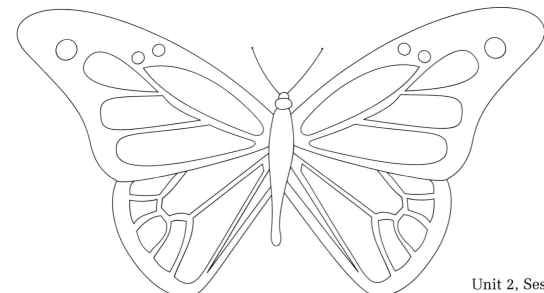

PRAYER

You have learned more of our special faith prayer, the Apostles' Creed. Pray these words now. Pause after each sentence to tell Jesus what the words mean to you.

He suffered under Pontius Pilate,
*   was crucified, died, and was buried.*
He descended to the dead.
On the third day he arose again.
He ascended into heaven,
*   and is seated at the right hand of the Father.*
He will come again to judge the living and the dead.

Spend a few quiet moments with Jesus. He loves being with you. You are content in each other's company. If there is something you want to ask Jesus, or tell him, do it now. Listen to him.

Faith Summary

Jesus came to reveal God's love. He suffered and died for us. By the power of the Holy Spirit he rose from the dead. Through his death and resurrection we are saved.

Word I Learned

Paschal Mystery

Ways of Being Like Jesus

Before Jesus died, he asked the Father to forgive his enemies. You are like Jesus when you forgive those who do you wrong.

With My Family

Put your family members' wishes before your own. Let someone else decide which television show to watch. Help take care of a younger brother or sister without being asked.

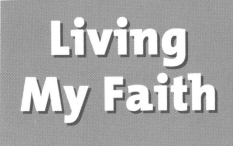

 PRAYER

Jesus, Lord, thank you for giving your life to save me. Help me to live my life to help others.

My Response

What will you do this week to show that you will live your life in service to others? Draw a picture.

Focus on Faith

A Moment of Grace

Sitting at a picnic table in a state park, a father and his daughter had time to talk alone. The father was moved to share with his daughter his sorrow for some things he had said to her that had been hurtful and harsh. The daughter listened with a forgiveness too deep for words. Their lives changed in that moment. The father recognized his responsibility. The daughter recognized her father's sincerity and forgave him. This was a moment of grace. This was a moment in which the new life given to us by Jesus and celebrated in the sacraments was realized.

Dinnertime Conversation Starter

Discuss with your children what it is like to ask for forgiveness from someone you have hurt in some way. Talk with family members about the importance of being sincere when apologizing and accepting apologies.

The Holy Resurrection, Nana Quparadze

In Your Parish

This is a good opportunity to discuss the Stations of the Cross with your child. You might use a children's version of the stations to read and reflect on together or refer to the back of your child's book. Point out that many people have visited Jerusalem and followed Jesus' footsteps along the way of the cross. Show your child the Stations of the Cross in your church.

Hints for at Home

If we live lives of service to others, we will be ready to face Jesus when he judges the living and the dead at the end of time. Trace your child's foot on a piece of construction paper. Help your child identify ways to follow Jesus' example. Write these on the foot. Cut out the outline and attach it to the refrigerator with a magnet as a reminder of ways to follow in Jesus' footsteps.

Focus on Prayer

Your child has learned more of the Apostles' Creed. Pray this prayer with your child. Point out how the part that he or she has just studied, the fourth through eighth sentences, summarizes our Catholic beliefs about Jesus' death and resurrection.

Review

Jesus' life on earth is a loving example of how we should live.
Jesus invites us to be helpers in the Kingdom of God. We do this
by answering his call to serve and care for others.

PRAYER

*Jesus, my teacher, help me learn from the example of your life so that
I can learn to show my love for others.*

Faith Summary

Through his parables Jesus teaches us how to find God in our everyday lives. As God's Son he shows us how to love God and others by the example of his own life.

Jesus calls us to obey the Ten Commandments and challenges us to do more. Grace helps us to become followers of Jesus.

The apostles and disciples accepted Jesus' mission to proclaim God's kingdom. Jesus also invites us to proclaim the kingdom and serve others in his name.

Jesus suffered and died for us. Through his life, death, and resurrection we are saved.

A Symbol of New Life

Each of the pictures above is a symbol of new life or resurrection. Can you tell why?

Sometimes we think of the cross as a symbol of being saved. Why do you think the cross makes us think of being saved?

Crossword Puzzles

Look back on the unit to find words that match the clues below. Write the words on the crosses. Talk about these words.

Across: story told by Jesus

Down: place where monks live, work, and pray

Across: fisherman who followed Jesus

Down: type of seed that grows into a large bush

Across: what Jesus sent his followers on

Down: special friends of Jesus

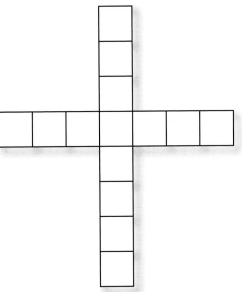

What Does Jesus Do?

Inside each of these shapes is a symbol or picture of something Jesus does for us. Can you match the action words with their symbols? Write the words on the lines near the shapes. Then talk about how we know that Jesus does these things for us.

loves	calls	teaches	saves	helps

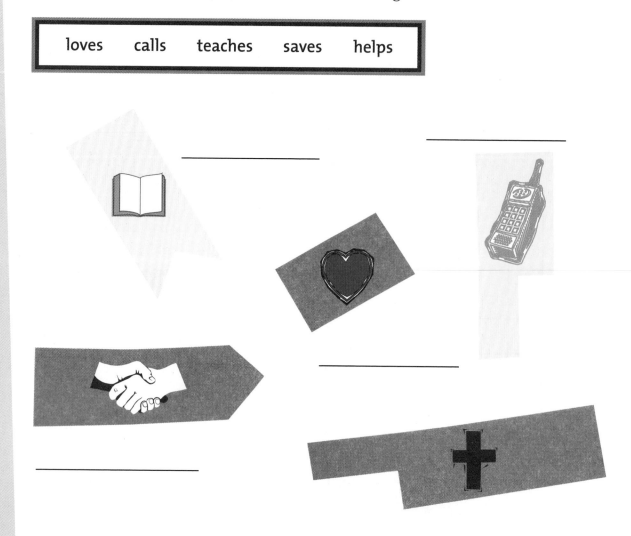

Create Your Cross

These shapes can be put together to make a cross. Carefully cut out the pieces. Use all five of them to make a cross.

PRAYER SERVICE

Leader: *The Lord has done wonderful things for us. Let us sing praise to God.*

Group A: *Sing to the Lord a new song; everyone on earth, praise the Lord.*

Group B: *Sing to the Lord, bless his name; day after day say that the Lord has saved us.*

Group A: *Tell all the people in every nation, the Lord does wonderful things for us.*

Group B: *For the Lord is great and worthy of praise; we respect him above all else.*

[adapted from Psalm 96:1–4]

Leader: *Let us close by proclaiming Christ's death and resurrection.*

All: *Christ has died, Christ is risen, Christ will come again.*

Living My Faith

Ways of Being Like Jesus

You are like Jesus when you show concern for others. If someone seems to be having trouble, ask how you can help. Take a few minutes to listen to him or her and offer your support.

With My Family

Think of a small activity you can do with a relative. Perhaps you can do a craft or an art project.

 PRAYER

Jesus, my Savior, thank you for calling me to love God and others. Help me follow your invitation to spread God's word.

My Response

Jesus teaches us that all our actions are important, no matter how small. Think of one thing that you can do to make someone's life a little easier. Write a sentence about it.

_____

_____

Community of Jesus

Saint Katharine Drexel

Katharine Drexel followed the path of Jesus. She gave away her wealth to help Native Americans and African Americans.

Saint Katharine Drexel

Katharine Drexel was born to a wealthy family in Pennsylvania in 1858. Her parents taught her to use her wealth to help others.

After Katharine's parents died, she traveled around the country. She saw the suffering of the Native Americans and African Americans. She decided to use her fortune to help them.

Katharine asked Pope Leo XIII to send missionaries to help people in need. The pope replied, "Why don't *you* become a missionary?" She knew she was being challenged to do more. She started the Sisters of the Blessed Sacrament.

Mother Katharine Drexel began about 60 schools and missions in the United States. She spent many millions of her own money to help others. Katharine Drexel accepted Jesus' mission by giving up her wealth and following him. Her feast day is March 3.

Jesus Sends the Holy Spirit

Think of the special celebrations and activities in your life. What events have filled you with energy and excitement?

 PRAYER

Jesus, open my heart to receive the grace of the Holy Spirit.
Help me to use well the gifts he brings.

A Wind from Heaven

After Jesus' life on earth ended, his disciples gathered in Jerusalem during the celebration of Pentecost. Suddenly the sound of a strong wind filled the house. Tongues of fire appeared over each person's head. Jesus' disciples were filled with the Holy Spirit.

Hearing the noise, a crowd gathered and began talking and shouting. They were confused. People from all over the world were there. They spoke many different languages. Yet each heard the disciples' message in his or her own language. They asked one another, "What does this mean?"

adapted from Acts of the Apostles 2:1-12

The Pentecost, El Greco

Accepting Jesus' Mission

The disciples realized that the Holy Spirit had come to them, just as Jesus had promised. They were excited. The Holy Spirit gave them strength to continue Jesus' mission. The disciples were ready to tell people all over the world about Jesus. Each would be a **witness** to Jesus.

How can you be a witness to Jesus? Share your ideas.

The Holy Spirit Builds the Church

At Pentecost, the Holy Spirit gave the disciples the strength to continue Jesus' mission. The Holy Spirit began building the Church. Today, the Spirit builds the Church through us, filling it with life. The power of the Holy Spirit is like the wind—though we cannot see it, we can feel its strength. The Holy Spirit gives us strength to continue Jesus' mission in our lives.

The Holy Spirit Is With Us

Jesus sent the Holy Spirit to be with us and to guide us. The Holy Spirit helps us to live prayerful lives. The Holy Spirit will stay with us on the journey that leads us to heaven.

Witnesses to Jesus

The Holy Spirit helps each of us to be a witness to Jesus Christ. Katharine Drexel was a witness when she gave away her wealth to help others. The disciples were witnesses when they spread Jesus' message around the world. Finish the sentence to show how you can be a witness to Jesus Christ.

I can be a witness to Jesus Christ when I _____

_____

Sacred Site

Katharine Drexel gave her fortune to help others and followed Jesus. She is remembered at the Shrine of Saint Katharine Drexel in Bensalem, Pennsylvania. It is also the Motherhouse of the Sisters of the Blessed Sacrament, the order of sisters that she began.

The Fruits of the Holy Spirit

Just as the Holy Spirit came to the disciples at Pentecost, he also comes to us. The Holy Spirit gives us the help we need to follow Jesus and to serve God and others. When our actions are guided by the Spirit, the result is the Fruits of the Holy Spirit.

love
patience
kindness
joy
peace
gentleness
generosity
faithfulness
self-control

The Spirit in Our Actions

The Fruits of the Holy Spirit are listed above. Read each one and talk about its meaning. Then choose one of the Fruits of the Holy Spirit. Write how it can be seen in your actions by finishing this sentence.

The fruit of _____ can be seen in my

actions when I _____

Reading God's Word

The fruits of the Spirit are love, joy, peace, patience, kindness, generosity, faithfulness, gentleness, and self-control.

adapted from Galatians 5:22-23

People all over the world have prayed this prayer for a very long time. Invite the Holy Spirit into your heart. Think about what you are praying as you say these words.

Prayer to the Holy Spirit

Come, Holy Spirit, fill the hearts of your faithful.

And kindle in them the fire of your love.

Send forth your Spirit and they shall be created.

And you will renew the face of the earth.

Lord,

by the light of the Holy Spirit

you have taught the hearts of your faithful.

In the same Spirit

help us to relish what is right

and always rejoice in your consolation.

We ask this through Christ our Lord.

Amen.

Now take a few minutes to thank Jesus for sending the Holy Spirit to you.

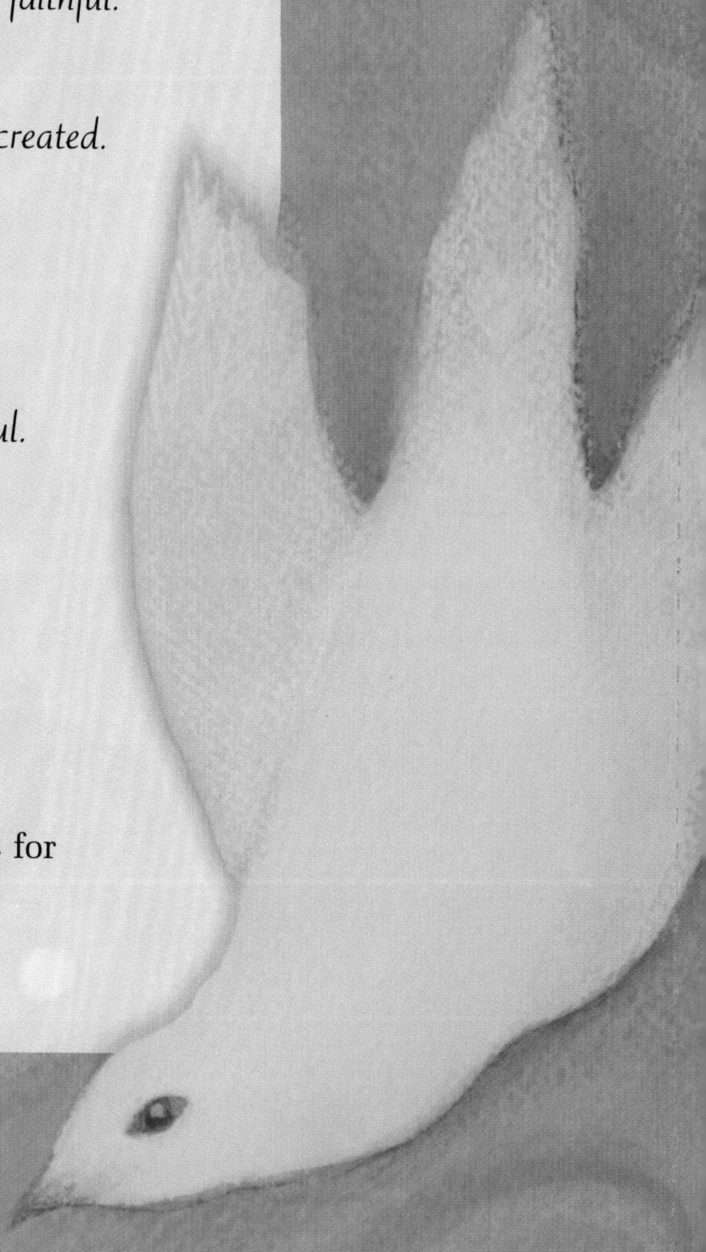

Faith Summary

Jesus sent the Holy Spirit to help his disciples carry out his work. The Holy Spirit helps us to be witnesses to Jesus and to lead prayerful lives.

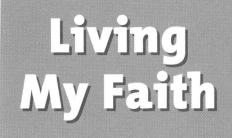

Living My Faith

Word I Learned

witness

Ways of Being Like Jesus

You can continue Jesus' mission by showing kindness to others. Be kind to someone who needs a friend by inviting him or her to play or to sit beside you at lunch.

With My Family

Show your family that the Holy Spirit helps you show your love. Be patient, even when it is hard. Keep your temper when you are upset. Show generosity by giving your time to help a brother, sister, or friend with homework.

PRAYER

Jesus, my helper, thank you for sending the Holy Spirit to support me on my journey. Help me to appreciate the presence of the Spirit in my life.

My Response

What will you do this week to practice gentleness and self-control? Write a sentence or draw a picture.

Focus on Faith

Saint Katharine Drexel Follows the Spirit

Saint Katharine Drexel came from a wealthy family. Her parents taught her that with wealth came responsibility. On a visit to Rome, she asked Pope Leo XIII to send missionaries to help those who were poor. The pope asked her why she didn't become a missionary. Katharine responded to the challenge of the pope and the call of the Holy Spirit. She dedicated her life to people in need and used her inherited wealth to help them.

Dinnertime Conversation Starter

Katharine Drexel learned about responsibility from her parents. Share with your child ways in which you or your family can responsibly assist less fortunate people in your community.

Spirituality in Action

Help your child to be aware of the presence of the Holy Spirit in his or her life. The Spirit's presence in our lives manifests itself in our behavior. By reading to a younger brother or sister, your child shares the generosity of the Holy Spirit. By being happy and making others happy, your child shares the joy of the Holy Spirit. Help your child recognize the work of the Holy Spirit in his or her life.

St. Katharine Drexel, Robert Lentz

Focus on Prayer

Your child has prayed the Prayer to the Holy Spirit. You will find this prayer at www.FindingGod.org. Pray this prayer with your child.

Our Catholic Heritage

Mother Katharine Drexel founded the Sisters of the Blessed Sacrament in 1891. Their work continues today. Their primary mission is to serve the needs of Native Americans, African Americans, and Haitians. Information about their educational and social work can be found on their Web site at **www.katharinedrexel.org**.

The Catholic Church

What symbols do you see every day? What symbol would you use to represent yourself?

PRAYER

Jesus, my Savior, show me how to follow you. I want to grow closer to you.

Peter and the Church

Peter said he believed Jesus was the Messiah. Jesus replied, "Peter, you are the rock upon which I will build my church. Even death will not destroy it. I will give you the keys to the kingdom of heaven."

adapted from Matthew 16:18-19

Symbols of Peter

The rock and the keys are symbols of Saint Peter. What do you think of when you see a rock? What do keys make you think of? Write your ideas on the lines and share them. Then talk about why these things remind us of Peter.

A rock makes me think of Church.

Keys make me think of heaven,

Did You Know?

Peter's name means "rock." Jesus named him this because he knew Peter would be a strong leader of the Church.

Serving the World in God's Name

The Church is the sign that we are one with the Father, Son, and Holy Spirit. Jesus chose Peter and the other apostles to lead the Church. Today the pope, who is the **Vicar of Christ,** leads the whole Church. The bishops teach, guide, and lead the Church in their areas. They appoint **pastors** to lead each parish. Together these leaders serve the Church as we share our faith and sacraments.

guy 1 *guy 2* *guy 3*

Leading the Church

Can you name your Church leaders? Write their names below. Ask for help if you need it.

My Church Leaders

Pastor _guy 1_____

Bishop _guy 2_____

Pope ___gu 3_____

Reading God's Word

Jesus asked Peter for the third time, "Do you love me?" Peter was hurt that Jesus had asked him three times. He said to Jesus, "Lord, you know everything. You know that I love you." Jesus answered, "Feed my sheep."

adapted from John 21:17

A Much Loved Leader

Pope Blessed John XXIII was one of our most beloved popes. Born Angelo Roncalli, he grew up on a small farm in Italy. He had twelve brothers and sisters. Angelo became a priest, spreading God's love as a teacher. He was elected pope in 1958, at age 76, and took the name John.

Pope John XXIII cared for people all over the world. He wanted all Christians, as well as people of all other religions, to understand one another. He was loved all over the world for his warmth, kindness, and sense of humor.

Soon after John was elected pope, he began his work reforming the Church. In 1962, he gathered Church leaders for the Second Vatican Council, which renewed the Church. Less than a year later, he died of cancer. Pope John Paul II declared him to be Blessed in 2001. This is the second step in becoming a saint. Pope Blessed John XXIII's feast day is June 3.

Our Holy Catholic Church

The Church can be both seen on earth and felt in our hearts. This is why we call the Church the **Mystical Body of Christ.** The Church has four important qualities, or marks:

*The Church is **one.*** We have one Lord and we share one faith. We receive one life in the Holy Spirit.

The Church is holy. The Father, Son, and Holy Spirit are holy. In the sacraments, we receive all we need to make us holy.

The Church is catholic. Catholic means universal. Jesus told the apostles to teach all nations. The Church reaches out to all.

*The Church is **apostolic.*** Jesus founded the Church with the apostles. The pope and bishops continue their mission today.

The Church is one, holy, catholic, and apostolic. These are the **Marks of the Church.**

Link to Liturgy

At Mass we pray for the Church and for our leaders, the pope and our bishop, during the eucharistic prayer. Listen for the names of your Church leaders during this prayer.

PRAYER

This last part of the Apostles' Creed states more of the things we believe. Notice them as you pray.

I believe in the Holy Spirit,
the holy catholic Church,
the communion of saints,
the forgiveness of sins,
the resurrection of the body,
and the life everlasting. Amen.

Jesus knows what is in your heart. Be still with him for a few moments. Tell him that you believe. Ask him to strengthen your belief.

Faith Summary

Jesus chose Peter and the apostles to be the leaders of the Church. The bishops and pastors, with the pope as their head, are today's leaders. Jesus calls us to be part of the Church community.

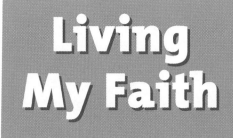

Words I Learned

apostolic   Marks of the Church   Mystical Body of Christ

one   pastor   Vicar of Christ

Ways of Being Like Jesus

Jesus asked the disciples to spread God's love through the Church. You can be like Jesus by sharing in the Church community and taking part in parish activities.

With My Family

Be an active member of the Church community with your family. Go to Mass together. Celebrate the sacraments as a family.

 PRAYER

Jesus, thank you for calling me to your Church. Support me as I follow the example of my Church leaders to serve others.

My Response

What will you do as a part of your parish community this week? Perhaps you will sing in the children's choir or help make a banner for your church. Draw a picture.

Tears of Saint Peter, El Greco

Focus on Faith

Jesus Calls Us to the Catholic Church

Choosing a name for a child takes thought. On the day of the September 11, 2001, tragedy, one couple named their newborn son Lucas. They did so because the name means "bringer of light." His name was a prayer for him and for the world too. Jesus also knew the importance of names. He saw in Simon the person of strength he needed to lead his disciples. So Jesus renamed Simon Peter, which means "rock," the rock on which Jesus could build the Church. Peter, a man who loved greatly and sometimes failed miserably, was also capable of change and growth. He was the kind of man Jesus needed.

Dinnertime Conversation Starter

Jesus saw Peter as the "rock." What image would Jesus use to describe individual members of your family in regard to their mission in the Church? The heart? The doorway? The mountain?

Our Catholic Heritage

Pope Blessed John XXIII, one of the most popular popes of modern times, was pope from 1958 to 1963. He convened the Second Vatican Council in 1962 to renew the Church. Two outcomes of the council include Mass in the language of the people and greater lay participation in the Church.

Spirituality in Action

Encourage your child to take part in special children's activities in your parish, such as children's liturgies or a young people's choir. Help him or her to learn the names of the pope and the local Church leaders.

Focus on Prayer

Your child has learned the entire Apostles' Creed. Pray this prayer with your child and discuss its meaning.

The Church Prays

What are some signs you see in your daily life?

What are the signs that are special to your family?

PRAYER

*Jesus, Lord, help me to be aware of your presence in the sacraments.
Help me to grow in my love of God.*

Jesus and the Roman Officer

Jesus went to the town of Capernaum. A Roman officer there had a servant who was very sick. When the officer heard about Jesus, he sent men to ask Jesus to save the servant's life. They urged Jesus, "Please do this for him. This man loves our nation, and he has helped us." Jesus went with them.

As they neared the house, the officer sent friends to tell Jesus, "Lord, do not trouble yourself. I am not worthy to have you enter my house. Just say the word and let my servant be healed."

adapted from Luke 7:1-7

Link to Liturgy

We say words like these before we receive Holy Communion at Mass. We say, "Lord, I am not worthy to receive you, but only say the word and I shall be healed."

A Man of Great Faith

The officer knew that he could order his soldiers to do something far away. In the same way, he believed Jesus could send his power to heal someone far away. Jesus was amazed when he heard this. He said, "I have never found such faith, even in Israel." The officer's friends returned to find the servant healthy.

adapted from Luke 7:8-10

Jesus Reaches Out to All

The officer had never met Jesus, but he had faith in Jesus. Jesus cared greatly for the Roman officer. Jesus showed that his mission was to all people. He showed that he could reach out to all people across time and space.

How can you show you care for all people as Jesus does?

Jesus Is Present at Mass

Just as Jesus reached out from a distance to heal the servant, he reaches out to be with us at Mass. He is present in the priest, in the people gathered, and in the Scriptures. Jesus Christ is especially present in the consecrated bread and wine.

Jesus Christ reaches out to us through all the sacraments. They help us to grow in faith and live as God wants us to. Through the Holy Spirit, Jesus Christ is present to us in the sacraments.

Signs of Grace

The sacraments are outward signs of the grace we receive from God. We are immersed in water or have it poured on us as a sign of Baptism. Bread and wine are signs of the Eucharist.

The Church gives us other signs, called **sacramentals.** They are not sacraments, but they help us grow in faith. Sacramentals can be objects, such as crosses or holy water. They can also be actions, such as the **blessing** of a person or place.

Gifts from God

God has given us many special gifts. Use what you have learned to finish each sentence. Fill in the puzzle with the missing words. Then unscramble the circled letters to find another special gift from God. Write that word in the sentence next to the puzzle.

1. Jesus was amazed by the soldier's _____.

2. An object such as a _____ is an example of a sacramental.

3. One type of sacramental is the _____ of a person or place.

4. Bread and water are signs of the _____.

5. A _____ is a sign of the grace we receive from God.

God's gift of

_____

helps us to live

as Jesus did.

Reading God's Word

Jesus was asked when the Kingdom of God would come. He answered, "No one will announce, 'Look, here it is,' or 'There it is.' For behold, the Kingdom of God is among you."

adapted from Luke 17:21

PRAYER

Think about the day Jesus healed the Roman officer's servant. Imagine that you are with the people following Jesus that day. You watch and listen as men approach Jesus and speak to him. What are they saying to him? What are the people around you saying?

Imagine Jesus turning toward you after he hears the officer's reply. What does he tell you? What do you say to Jesus?

Now spend a few moments with Jesus. Ask him to strengthen your faith through the sacraments. Thank him for his presence in the sacraments. Thank him for caring for you. Tell him how you will help him to care for others. Ask Jesus to help you remember he is always with you.

Faith Summary

Jesus gives us the sacraments to help us grow in faith. Through the Holy Spirit, Jesus Christ is present in the sacraments.

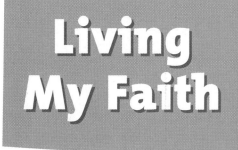

Words I Learned

blessing   sacramental

Ways of Being Like Jesus

Jesus reached out to all people, not just those who were like him. You can be like Jesus when you reach out to someone who is different from you.

With My Family

Jesus shares himself with us in the sacraments. Share yourself with your family by talking to them about yourself. Show your interest in them by listening to them.

PRAYER

Dear Jesus, thank you for giving me the sacraments. Help me to be open to the grace of the Holy Spirit, so I can show my love for God and others.

My Response

What will you do this week to celebrate the grace you receive in the sacraments? Will you help someone at school who is not just like you? Draw a picture.

Focus on Faith

Jesus Is With Us

Many of us wonder what it would have been like to meet Jesus in person. We would have liked to hear him speak and to experience his healing touch. The writers of the Gospels felt the same way. When the Gospels were written, two or three generations had passed since Jesus' life, death, and resurrection. People were feeling more removed from Jesus. Luke dealt with the issue by telling the story of the Roman officer who had asked Jesus to heal his servant from a distance. He trusted that Jesus' healing power would overcome any limitations. In response, Jesus healed the servant and praised the officer for his faith. Luke's Gospel is telling us that Jesus is alive. Through his resurrection and ascension Jesus lives with his Father and shares his continuing presence with us in the sacraments.

Dinnertime Conversation Starter

It is easy to forget that we meet Jesus in one another. Ask your child what person he or she encountered today who made Jesus more present. Share your own experience as well.

Spirituality in Action

Help your child to understand that Jesus reaches out across time and space to all people through us. We help Jesus care for others. Encourage your child to help his or her peers, regardless of differences. Suggest that he or she try to make a new friend of a different background at school or in your neighborhood.

Hints for at Home

Make the reception of the sacraments a very special celebration in your home. When there is a wedding in your family, remind your child that this

is the Sacrament of Matrimony. If an elderly person is sick, talk about the Anointing of the Sick. Encourage appreciation of the Sacrament of the Eucharist by doing something special after Sunday Mass, like going out for breakfast or having a special snack at home.

Focus on Prayer

Your child has reflected on the great faith of the Roman officer whose servant Jesus healed from a distance (Luke 7:1–10). You may want to read this story together. Point out that we, too, tell Jesus that we are not worthy to receive him when we receive Holy Communion. We say, "Lord, I am not worthy to receive you, but only say the word and I shall be healed."

Mary Is Holy

Mothers are very special people. They protect us and guide us.
What are some of the other qualities of a mother?

PRAYER

*Jesus, help me to follow the example of Mary, your mother,
so that I can grow in faith and love.*

A Gift From God

Keisha's house was full of excitement. The whole family was preparing for the birth of its newest member. Gifts were everywhere. Keisha asked her mother, "Which gift do you like best?" Her mother smiled. The greatest gift, she said, was the one growing inside her. Her child was a blessing from God.

Mary Is Blessed by God

When Mary learned that God would give her a child, she also knew that she had been blessed. The angel Gabriel appeared to Mary and said, "Hail Mary, full of grace, the Lord is with you!" Mary was so excited that she had to share the news with her family. She visited Elizabeth, her cousin. Elizabeth said to Mary, "Blessed are you among women, and blessed is the fruit of your womb."

These are the first words of the Hail Mary. Can you pray the rest?

Annunciation, Maurice Denis, 1913

Mary's Song of Praise

Mary and Elizabeth were overjoyed. They would both be blessed with special children. Elizabeth's child would be John the Baptist. Mary's child would be Jesus, the Son of God. Mary praised God by praying these words:

> "My soul praises the greatness of the Lord. My spirit finds joy in God my Savior. He has chosen and blessed me. God has done great things for me, and holy is his name! God helps the poor and feeds the hungry. He lifts up the lowly. He shows mercy to those who love him."
>
> *adapted from Luke 1:46-54*

We call this prayer the Magnificat. Like Mary, you can pray these words to thank God for all he has done for you. Ask God to help you to help others.

Mosaic of Mary (fragment)

Reading God's Word

Blessed are you who believed and trusted that what the Lord told you would really happen.

adapted from Luke 1:45

The Church Celebrates Mary

Mary celebrates the greatness of God in the Magnificat. She praises God for blessing her. Just as Mary praises God, the Church honors Mary. She is the Mother of God and the Mother of the Church. Mary shows us how to truly listen to God. She teaches us how to trust and believe. Mary is the best example of what it means to be a saint.

We Are All One

The Holy Spirit calls us to follow Jesus. We come together as the Church, especially in the Eucharist. Together with those who have died, we are one body, united before God. We call this one body the **Communion of Saints**.

Part of the Great Body

Close your eyes a moment. Imagine yourself gathered with the Communion of Saints. Write down your thoughts.

_____

_____

We Pray the Rosary

The **Rosary** helps us to honor Mary.
When we pray the Rosary, we
think about the special events,
or mysteries, in the lives of
Jesus and Mary. For example,
we think of the **Annunciation,**
when Mary learned she
was to be Jesus' mother.
We think of the **Visitation,**
when she visited her cousin
Elizabeth. While we think
about these joyful events, we
pray to God and honor Mary.

Look at the cross on the Rosary.
We pray the Sign of the Cross and the
Apostles' Creed when we hold the cross.
Look at the sets of ten beads each. We pray
the Hail Mary when we hold each of these
beads. Look at the beads in between the sets.
We pray the Lord's Prayer at the beginning
of the set and the Glory Be to the Father
at the end.

Did You Know?

When we pray the Rosary, we reflect on the lives of Jesus and
Mary as the Joyful, Sorrowful, and Glorious Mysteries and the
Mysteries of Light.

Let us pray together, reflecting on these special events in the lives of Jesus and Mary.

The Annunciation	The angel Gabriel tells Mary she will be Jesus' mother.
The Visitation	Mary visits her cousin Elizabeth.
The Nativity	Mary and Joseph go to Bethlehem, where Jesus is born.
The Presentation	Mary and Joseph bring Jesus to Jerusalem to be presented to God.
The Finding of Jesus in the Temple	Joseph and Mary find Jesus in the Temple talking with the teachers.

Faith Summary

The Church is united through the Eucharist in the Communion of Saints. We follow Mary's example of faith and love. She is the Mother of God and the Mother of the Church.

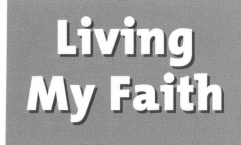

Living My Faith

Words I Learned

Annunciation   Communion of Saints   Rosary   Visitation

Ways of Being Like Jesus

Jesus loved his mother very much. Mary is a mother to us too. You can be like Jesus by loving Mary and following her example of faith and love.

With My Family

Ask your parents about the time they learned they would have a child. How did they prepare for your birth? Do something extra for them to thank them for caring for you.

PRAYER

Jesus, my guide, thank you for sharing your mother with me. Watch over me as I listen to God and trust in him as Mary did.

My Response

What will you do this week to show that you are a loving and trusting son or daughter? Draw a picture of what you will do.

Focus on Faith

The Rosary Helps Us to Pray

The most popular devotion in memory of Mary is the Rosary. The word *rosary* means "crown of roses," which reflects the idea of offering a gift of prayers. The Rosary emerged in medieval times as a form of prayer that people could use at any time or place. The Rosary is a meditative prayer on the mysteries that are scenes from the lives of Jesus and Mary. Praying the Rosary together will help your family to appreciate this way of relating to God.

Dinnertime Conversation Starter

What devotions or activities are part of your family's prayer tradition? Plan a way to integrate prayer into your next holiday celebration.

Female Saint with a Stag, Konrad Witz

Spirituality in Action

Mary has many names, such as Our Lady of Chiquinquira and Our Lady of Lourdes. Encourage your child to have a special devotion to Mary by creating a name for her as patron of your home. Examples of names could be Our Lady of the Household or Mary, Queen of the Family. Think of other possible titles and then, as a family, choose one.

Focus on Prayer

Your child has reviewed the Hail Mary and meditated on the Joyful Mysteries of the Rosary. Provide your child with his or her own rosary and emphasize that it is something special to have. Pray the Rosary together and talk about the events of each of the mysteries. Refer to www.FindingGod.org for help in praying the Rosary.

Our Catholic Heritage

In his document to the bishops called *Marialis Cultus,* Pope Paul VI talked about devotion to the Blessed Virgin Mary. He gave many examples in which he said that modern women would recognize what a strong person Mary was. He said that she is an example for men and women of our time, as "the disciple who works for that justice which sets free the oppressed and for that charity which assists the needy."

Review

Jesus calls us to be part of the Church community. He sends the Holy Spirit to build the Church through us. By praying and celebrating the sacraments, we are one body before God.

PRAYER

Jesus, Lord, teach me what it means to be a member of the Body of Christ. Teach me to appreciate all the help you give me on my faith journey.

Faith Summary

Jesus sent the Holy Spirit to help the disciples carry out his mission. The Holy Spirit brings life and strength to the Church.

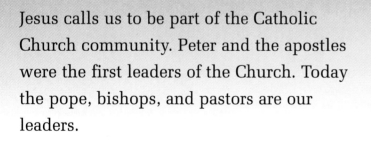

Jesus calls us to be part of the Catholic Church community. Peter and the apostles were the first leaders of the Church. Today the pope, bishops, and pastors are our leaders.

Jesus gives us the sacraments to help us worship God. In the celebration of the sacraments, Jesus is present to us through the grace of the Holy Spirit.

The Church is united before God in the Communion of Saints. Mary, the mother of Jesus and of the Church, is our model of a saint. We pray the Rosary to remember the lives of Mary and Jesus.

Who Am I?

We learned about the many helpers whom Jesus gives us as we grow in faith and love. Can you use the clues to name these helpers?

Holy Spirit   Pope   Pastor   Jesus Christ   Mary   Bishop

1. I am the Mother of Jesus. I love him and I love you.
   Who am I? _____

2. I came to Jesus' followers on Pentecost. I bring life to the Church. Who am I? _____

3. I am a leader of the Church. I watch over many parishes.
   Who am I? _____

4. I am the leader of a parish. I help the people in my parish grow closer to God. Who am I? _____

5. I give myself to my followers in the celebration of the sacraments. Who am I? _____

6. I am the leader of the Catholic Church today. I am the Vicar of Christ. Who am I? _____

Each of these helpers guides us to be better Christians. In the hand, write the name of someone who is a special helper to you in becoming a better Christian.

_____

The Spirit Lights Our Way

The tongues of fire remind us of the Holy Spirit coming to Jesus' followers. Through the Spirit, the Fruits of the Holy Spirit can be seen in our actions. Under each of the smaller candles are letter clues to the Fruits of the Holy Spirit. Can you write the name of each of them? You may look back in Session 11 for help.

Now think about the many gifts God has given you. They may be those on the candles or they may be others. Perhaps you are good at listening or at fixing things. In the largest candle write a gift you feel is yours to share. Cut your candle out to use in the Prayer Service.

j__ __

p__ a c __

p a__ __ e n __ __

l__ v __

k __ __ d __ __ s __

PRAYER SERVICE

Leader: Let us praise God, who enlightens every heart, now and forever.

All: Amen.

Leader: Hold your candles high. May they remind you of the love of the Spirit. May you be guided by the Holy Spirit to accept his gifts and share them with others. We thank Jesus for sending the Holy Spirit to light our lives.

All: Amen.

Reader: A reading from the first letter to the Corinthians.

There are different kinds of spiritual gifts, but they come from the same Spirit. There are different ways to serve the Lord. We all do different things, but the same God helps each of us. The Spirit gives each of us gifts. We serve others in our own way, as we work with the same Spirit.

[adapted from 1 Corinthians 12:4-7,11]

The Word of the Lord.

All: Thanks be to God.

Leader: Let us end our prayer with the Sign of the Cross.

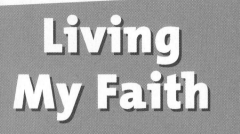
Living My Faith

Ways of Being Like Jesus

You can be like Jesus by helping with his mission of service to others. You are part of his Church community and you can follow Mary's example of faith and love.

With My Family

Celebrate the sacraments with your family. Pray with your family and celebrate the Eucharist together. Respect your parents as Jesus respected Mary and Joseph.

PRAYER

Jesus, Son of Mary, thank you for calling me to your Catholic Church. Watch over me as I grow in faith with the help of the Holy Spirit and our mother, Mary.

My Response

Tell how you will use the gift you wrote on your candle to help others. Write a sentence about it.

_____

_____

_____

Meeting Jesus

Saint Paul the Apostle
Saint Paul was called to be a follower of Jesus. He traveled to many countries to spread the Christian faith. In his writings, he teaches us to love God and one another.

Saint Paul the Apostle

We read about Saint Paul in the Acts of the Apostles. Paul was born in Tarsus, in what is now the country of Turkey. He went to school in Jerusalem and studied Jewish law. Paul did not believe that the followers of Jesus were faithful to Jewish tradition. Paul wanted to destroy the Church.

Paul was there when Stephen, a follower of Jesus, was killed because he was a Christian. Paul then went to Damascus to arrest more Christians. On the way, a bright light blinded him. He heard the voice of Jesus Christ, who had chosen him to become a follower. Paul changed his ways, regained his sight, and was baptized.

Paul made long journeys to places around the Mediterranean Sea to tell people about Jesus. He started churches in many cities. He wrote letters to the people to help them become better Christians. These letters

are found in the Bible. When we read them, we learn of Paul's love for Jesus. The feast of Saint Paul is June 29.

Sacraments of Initiation

Think of a time you were welcomed to a new place.
How did you feel? How did people make you
feel welcome?

 PRAYER

Jesus, Son of God, open my heart to the gift of faith I have received.

Philip and the Court Official

Many disciples traveled long distances to continue Jesus' mission. Philip was called to make one of these journeys.

Philip was traveling a desert road from Jerusalem to Gaza. He met a court official from Ethiopia. The official was returning home from Jerusalem. He was in his carriage reading the Scriptures.

St. Philip, Beauneveu

The Holy Spirit told Philip to join the official. Philip ran up to him and asked, "Do you understand what you are reading?" The official said, "How can I, unless someone teaches me?" He invited Philip to sit with him and teach him.

The man was reading about someone being silent as he was led to be killed. He read about a man being denied justice. He wondered who this man was.

adapted from Acts of the Apostles 8:26-34

A Joyful Acceptance

Philip told him the man was Jesus. As they traveled, Philip told the official all about Jesus.

Then they came to a stream. The official said, "Look, there is water. Why can't I be baptized?" They walked to the water and Philip baptized him. The official went joyfully on his way. Philip continued on his journey, spreading Jesus' message in each town he visited.

adapted from Acts of the Apostles 8:35-40

Welcome to the Church

Philip welcomed the official to the Church through Baptism. Imagine the official is a new member of your parish. What would you say to make him feel welcome? Write a message in the space below.

Dear New Member,

_____

_____

_____

Your friend,

_____

We Belong

Like the Ethiopian official, we are called to accept the gift of faith joyfully. We are called to form one family in Christ as members of the Church. We enter the Church, which is the **People of God,** by faith and Baptism. Through Baptism, original sin is forgiven. We are given sanctifying grace and we begin a new life.

Baptism is a gift from God. All people, no matter what their age or background, can enter God's family through Baptism. We pray for children who have died without Baptism. We trust in God's mercy and pray for them as members of God's family.

 Link to Liturgy

On special days, the priest invites us to renew our baptismal promises at Mass. Easter is one time we do this. On Easter we think about rising with Jesus to new life. When we renew our baptismal promises, we recommit our lives to God.

Christian Initiation

Through the Sacraments of Initiation—Baptism, Confirmation, and Eucharist—we receive the Holy Spirit. In Baptism we begin a new life in Jesus. At Confirmation we are anointed with holy oil and strengthened by the Holy Spirit. The Holy Spirit helps us to be witnesses to Jesus. In the Eucharist we receive the Body and Blood of Jesus Christ, which makes us one with him.

Welcome to God's Family

Say the name of the sacrament each person has celebrated.

1. The bishop anointed Luis's forehead with oil.

2. Caitlin was excited as she received Jesus Christ for the first time.

3. The priest immersed Eamonn in the water and prayed.

Reading God's Word

You have been called to live in hope as one body with one spirit.

adapted from Ephesians 4:4

PRAYER

Leader: We read in the letter to the Ephesians that we are called to live as one body and one Spirit. Let us answer God's invitation to be part of his family by expressing our belief in him.

Do you believe in God, the Father almighty, creator of heaven and earth?

All: *I do!*

Leader: Do you believe in Jesus Christ, his only Son, our Lord?

All: *I do!*

Leader: Do you believe in the Holy Spirit?

All: *I do!*

Leader: Thank God for making you part of the People of God. Ask him to keep making your faith stronger as you grow older. Thank him for making you one with him. Then spend a moment just loving him.

Faith Summary

Through the Sacraments of Initiation—Baptism, Confirmation, and Eucharist—we become members of the Church. We belong to the People of God. We are one family in Jesus.

Word I Learned

People of God

Ways of Being Like Jesus

You can be like Jesus when you are welcoming to others. Help people who are new to your class feel welcome by talking to them and offering your help.

With My Family

Treat your family members as part of God's family. Teach younger family members or friends about Jesus, as Philip taught the official.

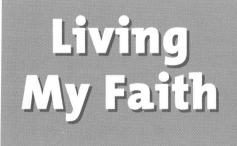

 PRAYER

Jesus, thank you for welcoming me to the People of God. Walk with me as I follow your example and spread your word.

My Response

What will you do this week to show that you belong to God's family? Write a sentence.

RAISING FAITH-FILLED KIDS
a parent page

Mosaic of Saint Paul, Ravenna, Italy

Focus on Faith

We Find Jesus Christ in the Church

Saul thought that he was doing something good by defending his faith. In doing so, however, he was persecuting Christians. As he traveled one day, he felt himself thrown to the ground and struck blind. A voice asked, "Why are you persecuting me?" It was the voice of Jesus Christ. On that day Saul became the apostle Paul, the great missionary to the Gentiles. Today Jesus is calling us to be members of the same Church. We celebrate our becoming members of the Church in the sacraments of Baptism, Confirmation, and Eucharist. Within the Church, we find our companions in faith on the journey to God.

Dinnertime Conversation Starter

Paul was quick to respond to Jesus' call. Discuss with your child the things in his or her life that make following Jesus difficult at times.

Hints for at Home

Talk to your child about the importance of godparents in the Sacrament of Baptism. You may want to have your child write a note to his or her godparents thanking them for what they have meant in your child's life. You could arrange a visit with them to talk about their memories of your child's Baptism.

Spirituality in Action

Help your child understand our call to belong to the People of God. Make an effort to meet other people in your parish. Treat them as family, always being friendly and respectful. Remind your child to treat everyone he or she encounters, such as a bus driver or a crossing guard, with respect.

Focus on Prayer

Your child has reflected on the Sacraments of Initiation, especially Baptism and Eucharist. Spend time talking with your child about these special events. Talk about the importance of thanking God for welcoming him or her into the Church at Baptism. Talk about thanking God for his gift of Jesus in the Eucharist.

Celebrating Reconciliation

Think of a time you asked
for forgiveness for something
you did wrong. How did
you feel when you were
forgiven?

PRAYER

*Jesus, my Savior, help me accept your gift of forgiveness.
I want to be at peace with myself and others.*

A Restless Start

Amanda was feeling grumpy. She didn't even smile when her mom said hello. At breakfast she sat down to eat without saying a word. Finally her mom said something to make her laugh, but Amanda started to cry. Then she told her mom what was wrong.

The third graders had gotten their math tests back the day before. Amanda had asked her friend Melissa what her grade was. Melissa trusted Amanda and told her. When Amanda learned that her own grade was higher, she made fun of Melissa. That made Melissa upset.

Amanda realized that she felt bad too. She knew she had hurt her friend. She didn't know what to do. She talked about it with her mom. Amanda said, "Mom, I'm going to tell Melissa I am sorry. I hope she will still be my friend."

What do you think Amanda said to Melissa? What do you think Melissa's reaction was? Do you think the girls remained friends?

A Peaceful Ending

Amanda told Melissa she was sorry for hurting her. At first Melissa was still angry. Then she realized that her friend was really sorry. Melissa said, "That's OK, Amanda. We can still be friends." They decided to study together for the next test. Maybe they could both get better grades.

Amanda felt so much better after making up with Melissa. But she knew she still had one more thing to do. She wanted to ask God to forgive her in the Sacrament of Penance. She confessed her sin to the priest and received absolution. Amanda felt at peace both with her friend and with God.

Reading God's Word

I will listen for the word of God. The Lord will give peace to his people, to those who have faith and trust in him.

adapted from Psalm 85:9

Peace Be With You

The disciples were gathered in a room. Suddenly the risen Jesus Christ came to them. He said, "Peace be with you." He showed them the marks from his crucifixion. The disciples were filled with joy at seeing Jesus. Jesus said to them again, "Peace be with you. As the Father has sent me, so I send you."

Then he breathed on them and said, "Receive the Holy Spirit. Those sins you forgive will be forgiven."

adapted from John 20:19-23

Jesus Christ gave the disciples two special gifts. He gave them peace to live happily together. He also gave them the authority to forgive sins. The priests who hear our confessions share these gifts. Through them, Jesus gives us peace and forgives our sins in the Sacrament of Penance.

The Peace of Forgiveness

People have been tempted to disobey God ever since Adam and Eve. After Baptism takes away original sin, we can still reject God by disobeying him and being self-centered. We call this **personal sin.**

There are two kinds of personal sin. When we totally reject God, we commit a mortal sin. Sins that are less serious are venial sins. God asks us not to form a habit of committing sins, even venial sins. But when we do sin, the Holy Spirit helps us to be sorry. Then we can confess our sins in the Sacrament of Penance and be at peace with God and ourselves, as Amanda was.

Jesus' Words of Forgiveness

Fill in the words of Jesus. Look back in this session for help.

1. _____ be with you.

2. As the _____ has sent me, so I send you.

3. Receive the _____ _____.

4. Those sins you _____ will be forgiven.

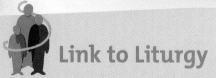

Link to Liturgy

We repeat Jesus' words during the sign of peace at Mass. We shake hands with one another and say, "Peace be with you."

PRAYER

Today let us reflect on Jesus' call to forgiveness. Think of times when you have sinned. Tell Jesus that you are sorry. Then pray the Act of Contrition.

Act of Contrition

My God,
I am sorry for my sins with all my heart.
In choosing to do wrong
and failing to do good,
I have sinned against you
whom I should love above all things.
I firmly intend, with your help,
to do penance,
to sin no more,
and to avoid whatever leads me to sin.
Our Savior Jesus Christ
suffered and died for us.
In his name, my God, have mercy.

As you go forth this week, thank Jesus for the gift of forgiveness. Ask Jesus to help you stay on the right path.

Faith Summary

When we turn away from God through personal sin, Jesus calls us to forgiveness in the Sacrament of Penance. We confess our sins, say we are sorry, and do penance for our sins. God always forgives us.

Word I Learned

personal sin

Ways of Being Like Jesus

You can be like Jesus when you forgive others who have hurt you. When you do wrong, be willing to say you're sorry.

With My Family

Think of something you have done recently that hurt a member of your family. Tell that person you are sorry.

PRAYER

Jesus, my friend, thank you for the gift of forgiveness. Help me to forgive others as you forgive me.

My Response

What will you do this week to share Jesus' gifts of peace and forgiveness? Draw a picture.

The Meeting of Esau and Jacob,
James Tissot

Focus on Faith

Healing Family Relationships

The story of Jacob's stealing his father's blessing is well known. Jacob disguised himself as his brother Esau and received the blessing from his nearly blind father, Isaac. Jacob then had to leave his family to escape his brother's anger. The story of Jacob's reconciliation with Esau is not so well known. When Jacob was returning to his old home with his family, he heard that Esau was coming with 400 men. Jacob feared the worst, but when Esau arrived, he ran to Jacob, embraced him, and kissed him. Jacob made restitution for the inheritance he had tricked Esau out of, and the break was healed. Family hurts are some of the most severe we can experience. As parents we can create an environment in which our children can learn to forgive and be reconciled with one another.

Dinnertime Conversation Starter

Families have habits just as individuals do. Has your family formed a habit of forgiveness? Discuss with them the freedom and joy that are the result of forgiving.

Our Catholic Heritage

The *Catechism of the Catholic Church* tells us that the Sacrament of Penance is known by many names. It is called the sacrament of conversion because Jesus' call to conversion is the first step in returning to God. It is

called the sacrament of confession because disclosure of sins to a priest is an essential part of the sacrament. It is called the sacrament of forgiveness because through the priest's absolution we receive pardon and peace. Finally, it is called the sacrament of reconciliation because through it, we are reconciled with God.

Spirituality in Action

Compliment your child when he or she acts as a peacemaker with other members of your family. Help him or her to say, "I'm sorry." Set an example if you do something wrong. Show by your example that you are a forgiving person.

Focus on Prayer

Your child has reflected on the words of the Act of Contrition. Pray this prayer with your child and talk about what it means. You can find this prayer at www.FindingGod.org. Encourage your child to pray for forgiveness for the sins he or she has committed and to seek reconciliation through the Sacrament of Penance.

Celebrating the Eucharist

Family meals are special celebrations. How does enjoying a meal with your family make it more special?

PRAYER

Jesus, my guide, help me to celebrate the Mass with love and reverence.

The Mass Makes Us One Family

Ricky had never been to a Mass celebrated in two languages. He was nervous. He knew only the few Spanish words Miguel had taught him. "Don't worry. Everything will be fine," Miguel whispered to his friend.

Miguel was right. As the people began to sing in Spanish, Ricky tried to sing along. Then the priest spoke. Sometimes the words were in English. Sometimes they were in Spanish. But Ricky always could tell what was happening. It was just like Mass at his parish!

Ricky looked around. In most ways this celebration was the same as his. When he received Holy Communion, he felt one with the people. No matter what language was spoken, he knew the people were all one family in Jesus Christ.

The Last Supper, Florence Martinez, 1942

Do This and Remember Me

Saint Paul told many people about Jesus' life. This is what he told the Church in a special letter, or **epistle,** about the Eucharist.

On the night when Jesus was betrayed, he took bread and gave thanks. Then he broke it and said to his disciples, "This is my body that I give to you. Do this and remember me."

After supper Jesus took the cup of wine. He said, "This cup is the new agreement made in my blood. As often as you drink it, remember me."

As often as you eat this bread and drink the cup, you proclaim the death of the Lord until he comes again.

adapted from 1 Corinthians 11:23-26

 **Reading God's Word**

I am the bread of life.

John 6:48

We Imitate Jesus

At the Last Supper, Jesus gave us a promise of his love. He called upon us to commit ourselves to God and to one another. The priest repeats Jesus' words at Mass. When we imitate Jesus in our lives, God's love is brought into the world.

At Mass Jesus Christ is present with us. He is present in the people gathered, in the priest who leads, in the Word of God proclaimed, and especially in the consecrated bread and wine.

The Mass is the central celebration of parish **worship.** It is the heart of the Church's life. It is offered for everyone, the living and the dead. An ordained priest leads us in the celebration of the Mass. We give thanks and praise to God for Jesus' life, death, and resurrection.

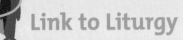

Link to Liturgy

The Eucharistic Prayer opens with joy in the words of the Preface. Everyone joins in by singing or saying, "Holy, Holy, Holy."

We Celebrate the Lord's Day

Sunday is the day on which we remember the Resurrection. It is the Lord's day. The Church celebrates by gathering for Mass and resting from work. We remember that we are all part of God's family. We are rich and poor, old and young. We come from all over the world. But we gather at God's eucharistic table as brothers and sisters.

Days of Celebration

As Catholics, we are called to celebrate the Eucharist on Sundays and Holy Days of Obligation. The Church asks us to receive Holy Communion as often as possible.

Draw a line from the dates to the holy days below. Then talk about how your parish celebrates these special days.

December 25	Mary, Mother of God
November 1	Birth of Jesus
January 1	All Saints Day

PRAYER

Jesus said, "I am the bread of life." Think of how much love is in these simple words. Jesus loves us so much that he gives us himself so that we may live.

Now think of Jesus' love in giving us the Sacrament of the Eucharist. Jesus is truly present in the consecrated bread and wine. Thank Jesus for giving himself to you in the Eucharist. Tell him what the gifts of his body and his blood mean to you.

Think of how close you are to him, especially when you receive Holy Communion. Thank Jesus for the wonderful gift of himself. Tell him how you will care for and share yourself with others as he does. Be still with Jesus in your heart.

Faith Summary

The Mass is the most important celebration in the Church. It is the heart of the Church's life. In the Eucharist we remember Jesus' life, death, and resurrection.

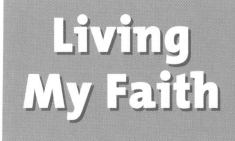

Words I Learned

epistle   worship

Ways of Being Like Jesus

You can be like Jesus when you treat others as brothers and sisters in God's family. Set an example for younger children by being friendly and kind to them.

With My Family

Jesus calls us to remember those who are poor when we celebrate the Eucharist. Your family can donate food to a food pantry. This will help other families to enjoy special meals together.

PRAYER

Jesus, thank you for giving me your self in the Eucharist. Thank you for making me one with God's family as I celebrate this sacrament.

My Response

What can you do this week to show that you are part of God's family, the Church? What small things can you do to treat others as brothers and sisters? Draw a picture.

Focus on Faith

Mass Begins at Home

Celebrating Mass on Sunday is central to our lives as Catholics. It is the celebration of our union with Jesus Christ and one another. We celebrate it best as a family when we create time for one another. On Sunday morning try to eliminate the ordinary distractions. Keep the television set, video games, and headphones off. Do some things differently, such as walking to church instead of driving. Arrange to have a special meal. Building family unity at home strengthens your union with Jesus.

Dinnertime Conversation Starter

As a family, plan what you can do to make Sunday special and different from any other day in the week.

In Our Parish

Take an active part in parish activities. If your parish has coffee and doughnuts after Sunday Mass, take part in this sharing activity. Treat other members of your parish as family by greeting them before or after Mass and by always being friendly and polite.

Our Catholic Heritage

On November 15, 2000, the United States Conference of Catholic Bishops issued a statement called "Welcoming the Stranger Among Us." It calls all members of the Church—clergy and laypeople— to a spirit of conversion, communion, and solidarity. It urges parishes to welcome newcomers genuinely. It suggests having common social events, international dinners, and multicultural parish feasts as means of leading people to

exchange and share cultures. There are proposals for prayers and liturgies. To read the bishops' statement in full, visit their Web site at **www.nccbuscc.org/mrs/unity.htm**.

Focus on Prayer

Your child has reflected on the wonderful gift Jesus gave to us in the Eucharist. He or she has reviewed the words spoken by Jesus to his disciples when he instituted the Eucharist. Help your child to understand how we remember this gift, especially during the Eucharist.

Christian Living

We each serve God in our own way. What ways of life are shown here? How do people with these jobs serve God and others?

PRAYER

Jesus, my brother, guide me in the search for a way of life that can help me serve God and others.

Out of This World

As the Solar System unit was ending for the third grade class, the best part was just starting. The class was divided into three teams. Each team would present a play filled with facts about the planets.

Sarah's team knew she was a good organizer. They chose her to be the director. Brooke and Andrew were good in science. They would get information and make sure everything was correct.

Yuki and Megan were already suggesting how they could be creative and factual: the team could travel to each planet and send postcards home. Suman and Adrian offered to build the spaceship. Vanessa said she'd use her new colored markers to draw pictures on the postcards. Leah loved to write in cursive, so she would write them. They all hoped to use their special gifts to make their plan work.

Do you think the children's ideas will work? Why or why not? How do you think you could have contributed to the project?

Many Gifts, One Spirit

There are different kinds of spiritual gifts. They all come from the same Holy Spirit. There are different ways to serve the same God. We each do different work, but the same God helps us. The Holy Spirit works in each of us to help us do things for the good of others.

Some of us can speak with knowledge and teach others. Some can heal sick people. The Holy Spirit decides which gifts to give us and calls us to use them.

adapted from 1 Corinthians 12:4-11

A Sharing Example

The students in the story all used their gifts to help their class project. In the same way, we must use our gifts to help our world. Draw a picture in the box of someone you know who shares his or her gifts in a special way. Talk about why you chose this person.

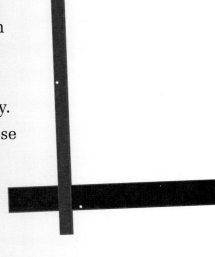

Link to Liturgy

At the dismissal of the Mass, the priest or deacon sends us forth to bring Jesus into the world by serving God and one another.

The Call to Share Our Gifts

God gives us many wonderful gifts. These are our special talents and abilities. The Holy Spirit calls us to share our gifts with the Church and community. We share Jesus' mission and act in his name. We each are called to a special **vocation,** or way of life.

Some men are called to be priests. Other men serve the Church by being ordained as deacons. They celebrate the Sacrament of **Holy Orders.**

Some men and women publicly dedicate their lives to serving God and the Church. Can you name someone you have learned about in this book who has done this?

Reading God's Word

Each one of you has received a gift. Share God's grace by using your gift to serve one another.

adapted from 1 Peter 4:10

Called to God's Service

Some men and women are called by the Holy Spirit to be married. They agree to live in faithful love in the Sacrament of **Matrimony.** Other people choose to remain single. Single people serve God in their lives and in the work they do in the world.

No matter what our vocation in life will be, we each are called to God's service. Have you imagined what your way of life might be as an adult? Talk about how through your choice you could share God's love.

Meet a Saint

Saint Andrew Kim Taegon was the first Korean person called to serve God as a priest. Andrew Kim was born to a noble family and became a Christian. When he was fifteen years old, he went to a seminary in southern China. He returned to Korea and began spreading God's word as a priest. Years later he and many others were martyred for their faith. The feast of Andrew Kim Taegon and his companions is September 20.

Saint Andrew Kim Taegon, Moon Hak-Jin

PRAYER

God has given each of us special gifts and talents. Think about your special talents. What things do you do very well? Do you use your talents at school? Do you use them to help at home?

Meet Jesus in your special place. Spend a few minutes talking with him about your talents. Tell him what you think your special abilities are. Thank him for giving these gifts to you. Tell him how you will share your gifts. Ask Jesus to help you to choose a vocation that will allow you to serve others.

Be still with Jesus for a few moments. Trust that Jesus will help you use your gifts and talents to do things well and to help others.

Faith Summary

God gives us special talents and abilities. The Holy Spirit calls us to share these gifts. We each are called to a way of life that will help us share God's love.

Words I Learned

Holy Orders   **Matrimony**   **vocation**

Ways of Being Like Jesus

You can be like Jesus when you use your special gifts to serve others. If you are gifted in a subject at school, you can share your knowledge. If you are gifted at sports, you can give pointers to someone who is struggling.

With My Family

Use your gifts and talents to be a contributing member of your family in your vocation as a son or daughter, sister or brother. You could use your talents to help cook, clean, or cheer someone up.

PRAYER

Jesus, my helper, thank you for helping me to recognize my gifts and talents. Support me as I try to use them to serve others.

My Response

What will you do this week to share your gifts and talents? Write a sentence to tell what you will do.

Focus on Faith

Signs of a Vocation

A young man had his parents puzzled. He would get enthusiastic about something for a while and then move on to something new. One summer it was landscaping; the next it was a passion for fixing cars. Another time he helped a friend build a house. He also faithfully attended Mass. When he told his parents of his intention to study for the priesthood, his father wondered whether this was just another short-term interest. The young man completed his studies and became a missionary priest. In a letter to his parents from overseas, he described how all of the skills he learned following his interests were being used in his mission. To what vocation is God calling your child? Look for the clues.

Dinnertime Conversation Starter

S hare with your child your interests as a youngster and how they influenced your choice of vocation. Listen as your child shares his or her interests.

St. Antonio María Claret, Maximino Cerezo Barredo

Spirituality in Action

Encourage your child to develop his or her special abilities. Help your child to realize that these are gifts from God. By your example, show him or her how to use one's talents to help others. Participate as a family in parish projects to help others.

Focus on Prayer

Your child has reflected on his or her special gifts and talents, thanking God for them and praying for the grace to use them in the service of others. Help your child to see how understanding one's talents can help in the choice of an appropriate vocation.

Hints for at Home

Talk to your child about the ways that people in the community serve God and others in their work. You could point out people you see in daily life and talk about each one's special gifts. A police officer keeps us safe. A mail carrier helps us to communicate with one another. A teacher helps us to learn and develop our gifts. A priest helps us to pray and to grow in faith. Help your child to understand the importance of each person's job.

Review

Through the sacraments, we become part of the People of God. We live as God's people by loving one another and sharing our gifts.

What gifts do you share?

PRAYER

Jesus, my Savior, help me to hear you and answer you, so that I may become what you want me to be.

Faith Summary

Jesus calls us to the joyful acceptance of the gift of faith. We celebrate this gift in the Sacraments of Initiation. Through them we become members of the Church, the one family of Christ.

When we fail to love God and others because of our sins, Jesus calls us to forgiveness through the Sacrament of Penance. God always forgives us when we are sorry for our sins.

The celebration of the Eucharist is at the center of parish life and worship. When we celebrate the Mass, we remember the sacrifice Jesus made for us.

We each receive different gifts from the Holy Spirit. We are called to share our gifts and talents with others. Jesus calls us to share them in a special way of life.

The Gift of Math

We learned that Saint Paul traveled to many countries to tell people about Jesus. When he left his new friends, he often wrote them letters to remind them of how they should live.

Use your math talent to solve these equations. Then use the letters to decode one of Paul's messages to his friends.

A = _____ 7 + 9

B = _____ 64 − 31

E = _____ 6 × 6

I = _____ 46 − 39

N = _____ 12 + 9

O = _____ 2 × 4

R = _____ 5 × 5

T = _____ 7 + 5

Saint Paul and his companions traveled by foot along the Appian Way in Italy. The route is still in use today.

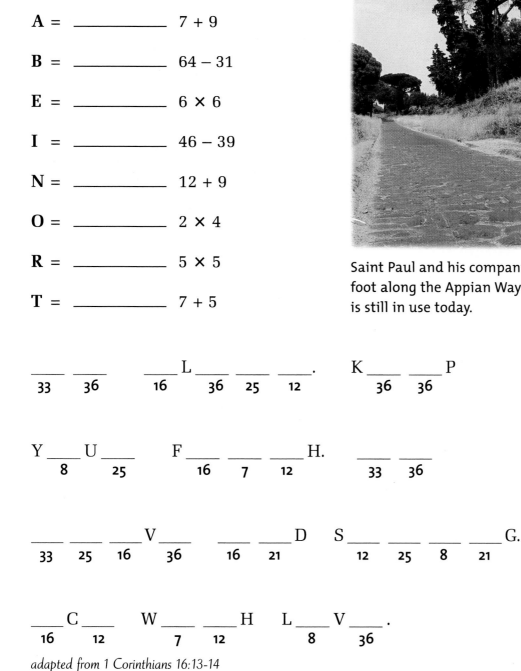

____ ____   ____ L ____ ____ ____.   K ____ ____ P
 33   36   16   36   25   12   36   36

Y ____ U ____   F ____ ____ ____ H.   ____ ____
   8   25   16   7   12   33   36

____ ____ ____ V ____   ____ ____ D   S ____ ____ ____ ____ G.
 33   25   16   36   16   21   12   25   8   21

____ C ____   W ____ ____ H   L ____ V ____.
 16   12   7   12   8   36

adapted from 1 Corinthians 16:13-14

A Message From Space

In this unit you read about a class project in which students pretend to visit space. Now imagine that those students have sent you this message from space. Some of the words were scrambled, and the ending was lost. Can you unscramble the words in the message? Can you finish the message with your own words?

Greetings From Outer Space!

We've met a group of friendly aliens. They have heart-shaped heads and stripes! They are very curious about us. Today we told them about the Catholic _____. We talked about
hcruCh

how we _____ God and celebrate the
hipswor

_____. Through _____, we told
scramtensa   **Btasmip**

them, we become part of the Church. God forgives our sins when we celebrate _____. We explained that we
ePancen

grow closer to Jesus when we celebrate the _____.
uchastEri

These aliens still have a lot to learn, though. They thought that we show that we are Catholics only by going to church. We told them that's not true. We also show that we are Catholics by

_____

PRAYER SERVICE

Leader: *The grace of our Lord Jesus Christ be with us all, now and forever.*

All: *Amen.*

Leader: *We have been called to live as God's people. Let us join hands as a sign of unity as we listen to these words. May we be guided by this message as we pray together.*

Reader: *A reading from the letter to the Ephesians.*

I ask you to live in a way that is worthy of God's people. Be humble, gentle, and patient. Love one another and live together in peace. You are all part of one body and one spirit of God. You were called to one hope. We have one Lord, one faith, one Baptism. There is one God and Father of all. He looks over us all, and he works through us and in us.

[adapted from Ephesians 4:1–6]

The Word of the Lord.

All: *Thanks be to God.*

Leader: *Let us end our prayer by praying the Sign of the Cross.*

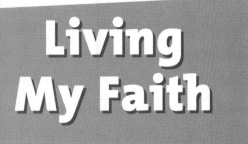
Living My Faith

Ways of Being Like Jesus

You can be like Jesus by sharing his mission of serving and caring for others. Live peacefully with the people you meet each day, such as your classmates.

With My Family

Remember that each member of your family has gifts to share. Tell each member of your family one gift he or she has been blessed with. Be a peacemaker by forgiving a family member or by saying you're sorry.

PRAYER

Jesus, Lord, thank you for your great gift of the sacraments. Help me to continue to grow in my faith and to choose a vocation in which I can serve God and others.

My Response

Think of a way that you can show your appreciation for the sacraments this week. Will you celebrate the Eucharist prayerfully and thoughtfully? Will you forgive a friend who has hurt you? Will you ask for forgiveness in the Sacrament of Penance? Draw a picture.

Living Like Jesus

Saint Monica

Saint Monica was a Christian, but her son was not. She loved her son and prayed for him for many years. Shortly before she died, her son was baptized. Saint Monica's son was Saint Augustine.

Saint Monica

Saint Monica was a Christian who wanted her family to share in Jesus' love. She patiently prayed for her husband, Patricius, and his mother, who were not Christians. Her prayers were answered when they were baptized. Her son Augustine, however, did not accept Jesus.

Monica loved Augustine very much. She never stopped praying for him, even though he grew up and moved away. She continued to hope, even when he made sinful choices. Her prayers were finally answered when Augustine was baptized at the age of 33. He later became a great bishop and teacher.

Monica is the patron saint of married women. She is a model for Christian mothers. She is our model when we pray for others to know Jesus. Her feast is August 27. The next day, August 28, is the feast of her son Augustine.

Monica and Augustine were born in Tagaste, which is now Souk Ahras, Algeria.

Faith, Hope, and Charity

We show our love for our neighbor by helping others. Think of a time you gave something to a person who needed it. How did you feel when you did this?

PRAYER

Jesus, my guide, show me how to live for others as you did. I trust in you and I want to be like you.

Trusting in God

Even when her son Augustine was far away, Saint Monica never stopped praying for him. She had **hope,** or trust in God. She believed that her son would one day choose to follow Jesus.

When Saint Paul was far from members of his Christian family, he trusted in God too. He wrote letters to his friends to praise them and to keep their faith strong. This is from a letter Saint Paul wrote.

We thank God always for all of you. We pray for you. We tell God about your faith, love, and hope in our Lord Jesus Christ. Know that God loves you and has chosen you to be his people.

adapted from 1 Thessalonians 1:2-4

Like Saint Monica, Saint Paul worked hard to keep his Christian family on the right path. He praised them for their faith, hope, and love. How has your family helped you follow Jesus?

We thank God always for all of you. We pray for you. We tell God about your faith, love, and hope in our Lord Jesus Christ. Know that God loves you and has chosen you to be his people.

Important Virtues

God gives us gifts called **virtues** to help us live good lives. Faith, hope, and **charity** are three of the most important virtues.

Faith helps us to believe in God. We need faith to be saved and to live as God wants. Hope helps us to trust that God will always be with us. With hope, we can be happy with God now and forever. We show charity when we love God above all things and love our neighbor as ourselves. Saint Paul tells us that charity, or love, is the most important virtue.

A Person of Virtue

There are many other virtues, such as friendliness and respect. Think of someone you know who is blessed with a virtue. Finish the sentence below by writing who that person is and what virtue he or she shows.

_____ *shows the virtue of*

_____

_____

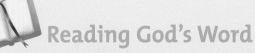 Reading God's Word

Faith, hope, and love each bring us closer to God; but the greatest of these is love.

adapted from 1 Corinthians 13:13

Symbols of the Virtues

The cross is a symbol of our faith. It reminds us that Jesus died
for our sins. An anchor is a symbol of hope for us. Just as an
anchor holds a ship, so does hope help us hold on to Jesus.
When we think of charity, or love, a heart comes to mind because
the heart is a symbol of love.

Matching Virtues

Which virtue is each person showing? Draw a line connecting
each virtue to its symbol. Draw another line from each symbol
to a sentence.

Charity	*Hope*	*Faith*

Martha trusts that God will always guide her.	Antoine shows his love by visiting a sick classmate.	Billy believes that Jesus lived and died for us.

Sacred Site

Many people visit the Church of Saint Augustine in
Rome. Saint Monica is buried in a chapel inside this
church. On the walls are pictures from the lives of
Augustine and Monica.

She Lived Like Jesus

Blessed Jeanne Jugan was a great example of the virtue of charity. She was born in a small fishing village in France in 1792. Her father died at sea when she was a child. Her family was poor, but her mother taught the children to live with faith and love for God.

When she was a teenager, Jeanne became a maid for a wealthy woman. The woman took Jeanne to visit those who were poor or elderly. As an adult Jeanne cared for poor and sick people in a local hospital.

One day she met an elderly blind woman who was sick and lonely. Jeanne brought the woman home with her and cared for her. Soon more elderly people came. More young women joined Jeanne. Together they took care of the elderly people.

Jeanne and her friends formed a community to help people who were poor or elderly. Others joined and they became the Little Sisters of the Poor. This community still serves the needs of elderly people all over the world.

The Little Sisters of the Poor collect donations to serve the needs of elderly people around the world.

PRAYER

Spend a minute quietly thanking God for the virtues you have been given. Thank him for your faith that helps you believe in him and all that he has told you.

Tell Jesus how hope helps you to trust in God's promises. Tell him how your faith and hope give you the strength to live a good life.

Now tell Jesus how you will show the virtue of charity. Tell him what you will do to help others.

Thank Jesus for guiding you. Ask Jesus to always help you remember he is with you.

Faith Summary

Faith, hope, and charity help us lead a Christian life. They are gifts from God called virtues. These virtues help us lead good lives.

Words I Learned

charity   hope   virtue

Ways of Being Like Jesus

You can live like Jesus when you show charity, or love for others. Be kind to a child you know who seems lonely, either at school or in your neighborhood.

With My Family

Talk with your family about ways you can brighten the lives of people who live alone or in a nursing home. Perhaps you can help with some housework, decorate a hallway, or bring food.

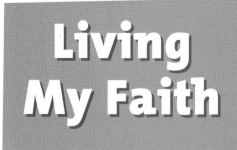

 PRAYER

Jesus, my example, thank you for sharing your life with me. Walk with me as I live my life of faith, hope, and charity.

My Response

What will you do this week to show the virtue of charity? Draw a picture.

a parent page

IL FAUT TOUJOURS DIRE: DIEU SOIT BÉNI

Jeanne Jugan, George Pinecross, 1942

Focus on Faith

Faith, Hope, and Charity

Blessed Jeanne Jugan (1792–1879) was born into a poor family in Brittany, France. In a local hospital she learned how to help those who were even poorer than she. Jeanne begged in order to help those who needed care. One businessman complained that she continued to bother him after he had given her money. Jeanne told him that the poor people she helped were hungry yesterday, are hungry today, would be hungry tomorrow, and that she would continue to beg for them. The businessman relented and became a regular contributor. Jeanne's community, the Little Sisters of the Poor, continues her work today. Its members are an example of how the decisions of a single person can lead to helping others globally.

Dinnertime Conversation Starter

Talk about a small decision that your family can make today to help others.

Our Catholic Heritage

The Little Sisters of the Poor, founded by Blessed Jeanne Jugan, are dedicated to helping people who are poor, sick, or elderly. From small beginnings, the religious community spread to thirty countries on five continents. Their service to elderly people is an example of the practice of the theological virtues of faith, hope, and charity. More information about the Little Sisters of the Poor is available on the community's Web site at **www.littlesistersofthepoor.org**.

Spirituality in Action

Consider visiting residents of an assisted living program and spending some time talking with them. Your child could engage in a few crafts beforehand and bring his or her creations to brighten the residents' rooms. Explain how such acts are an expression of Christian virtues. Helping your child do such things will bring happiness to him or her and pleasure to others.

Focus on Prayer

Your child has reflected on living the virtues of faith, hope, and charity. Help your child to understand that the grace of the Holy Spirit helps us to respond to God's call to live for others. Talk with him or her about various ways of practicing this virtue in his or her life.

Making Good Choices

Every day we make choices. Sometimes we need help to know what is right. What hard choice did you make this week? How did you decide what to do?

 PRAYER

Jesus, my helper, give me the grace to make good choices. I want to live for God and others like you did.

Jesus Is Tempted

The Holy Spirit led Jesus into the desert. Jesus didn't eat for 40 days and 40 nights. He was very hungry. The devil came and said to him, "If you are the Son of God, turn these stones into loaves of bread." Jesus said, "The Scriptures say that people do not live only on bread, but on every word that God speaks."

Then the devil took Jesus to the top of the Temple. He said to Jesus, "If you are the Son of God, throw yourself down. The Scriptures say that God will tell the angels to protect you." Jesus answered, "The Scriptures also say you shall not put God to the test."

The devil took Jesus to a high mountain and showed him all the kingdoms of the world. The devil said, "All these I shall give you if you worship me." Jesus said, "Go away, Satan! The Scriptures say that you shall worship God alone, and you shall serve only him." Then the devil left Jesus, and angels came and cared for him.

adapted from Matthew 4:1-11

Did You Know?

After Jesus was tempted in the desert, he went out into the world to begin teaching others.

Making a Moral Choice

The devil tempted Jesus with three hard choices. Jesus overcame these temptations by following the Father's will. Sometimes we must make hard choices too. With the help of the Holy Spirit, we can examine our choices. We ask ourselves the three questions below. Read the questions. Then read how Ana acted when she asked herself these questions. If we can answer yes to each question as Ana did, we know we have made the right choice.

1. *Is the thing I'm choosing to do a good thing?*

Ana finds a hat on the school playground. She likes the hat very much, but decides to bring it to the Lost and Found.

2. *Am I choosing to do it for the right reasons?*

Ana knows that the hat is not hers. The owner will be looking for it.

3. *Am I choosing to do it at the right time and place?*

Ana turns the hat in to the Lost and Found right away.

Ana made a good moral choice. She is happy. She did the right thing. The owner will be happy too. She can get her hat back.

Keeping the Commandments

God our loving Father gave us the Ten Commandments. They teach us how to live for God and others. They help us follow the **moral law,** rules that help us to do good and avoid evil.

Obeying God

When Jesus was tempted by the devil, he remembered the first commandment. He honored and obeyed God. The first three commandments teach us to honor God. This is what they tell us:

1. I am your God; love nothing more than me.

2. Use God's name with respect.

3. Keep the Lord's day holy.

Think about these commandments. What are some ways you can obey them?

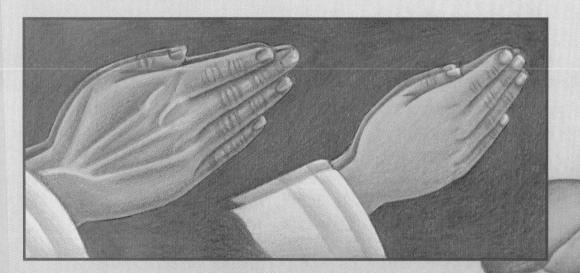

Reading God's Word

Whatever you do, in word or by your actions, do it in the name of Jesus, giving thanks to God the Father through him.

adapted from Colossians 3:17

Loving Our Neighbor

The first three commandments teach us about our relationship with God. The other commandments teach us how to live with our neighbor. This is what they tell us:

4. **Honor and obey your parents.**

5. **Treat all human life with respect.**

6. **Respect married life.**

7. **Respect what belongs to others.**

8. **Tell the truth.**

9. **Respect your neighbors and your friends.**

10. **Be happy with what you have.**

Obeying the Commandments

For each sentence below, write the missing word in the blank. Then write the number of the commandment the person in the sentence is obeying.

1. Peter obeyed his _____ when she said it was

   time for bed. _____

2. Mara goes to _____ with her family each

   Sunday. _____

3. Donnie told the _____ when the teacher asked if

   he had done his homework. _____

PRAYER

Each day, we remember to live our lives for God.
Each morning we can tell God we will live for
him by praying the Morning Offering. As you
slowly pray this prayer, think of what you will
give to God.

Morning Offering

*My God, I offer you my prayers, works, joys,
and sufferings of this day in union with the holy
sacrifice of the Mass throughout the world.*

*I offer them for all the intentions of your
Son's Sacred Heart, for the salvation of souls,
reparation for sin, and the reunion of Christians.
Amen.*

Now spend a few quiet moments with Jesus.
Tell him that you want to offer everything
you do to God. Ask Jesus to help you make
good moral choices each day. Be still.
Know that Jesus is with you.

Faith Summary

God gave us the Ten Commandments. They help us to follow the moral law. With the help of Jesus and the Holy Spirit, we can live our lives for God and others.

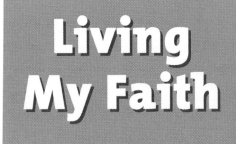

Word I Learned

moral law

Ways of Being Like Jesus

Jesus followed the Ten Commandments. Think of one of God's rules you sometimes have trouble keeping, such as telling the truth or obeying your parents. Ask yourself at the end of each day if you have followed that rule.

With My Family

Talk with your parents about a hard choice you have recently had to make. Ask them what they do when they have to make hard choices. Remember to ask them for advice when you have trouble deciding what to do.

 PRAYER

Jesus, my brother, thank you for showing me how to be a good person. Help me to follow your example of making good moral choices.

My Response

What will you do when you are faced with a moral choice? Will you ask yourself the three questions? Write a sentence or draw a picture.

RAISING FAITH-FILLED KIDS

a parent page

St. Monica, Lu Bro

Focus on Faith

Praying for Our Children

Saint Monica (332–387) was the mother of Saint Augustine. Wanting to follow his own desires, Augustine made bad decisions and pursued a worldly lifestyle. All during this time Monica loved and prayed for her son to make the right choices. She finally witnessed his conversion and saw him baptized at the age of 33. Augustine went on to become a bishop and a great Christian writer. Monica, the patron of married women and a model for Christian mothers, is a great example of persistence and faithfulness in prayer. As parents we recognize in Saint Monica a kindred spirit who prays with us that our children may make good choices and turn toward Jesus.

Dinnertime Conversation Starter

Talk with your child about the importance of praying often, even when it seems that God is not listening. What does your family want to pray for today?

Hints for at Home

Talk with your child about the importance of making moral choices. Be available to listen and help your child make decisions. With your child, examine the object of the decision, the intended action, and the circumstances of his or her choice to see whether all are good.

Spirituality in Action

Talk with your child about why rules are important. Review some rules that family members follow at home, and talk about how the rules help your family to function well. If there are no formal rules, brainstorm with your child to settle on a few rules that everyone should follow. Together, write down some rules as family commandments and hang them on the refrigerator.

Focus on Prayer

Your child is learning the Morning Offering. Help him or her to form a habit of praying this prayer each morning. You can find this prayer at www.FindingGod.org. Emphasize that your child can count on Jesus and you to help him or her grow closer to God.

Living as God's Children

How do you feel when your family is happy? What is one thing you do as a family to try to make your home a happy place?

PRAYER

Jesus, my friend, teach me how to share love and joy with my family and with others in God's family.

Getting Ready for the Party

"Come on down," Nina's mom called through her door. "We only have an hour before they come!"

Nina didn't feel like cleaning. She wanted to stay upstairs and play. Yet she knew the house might not get cleaned in time if she didn't help. She went downstairs to help her mother.

The rest of her family was already working hard. Dad was cleaning up the yard. Mom was cooking a big meal. Nina's sister Mara was setting the table. They were all excited about the big birthday party.

As Nina helped with the cleaning, she found herself getting excited too. It was fun to see her family working together. Cleaning the house didn't seem like such a chore. When her grandparents, aunts, uncles, and cousins arrived, she felt proud. She knew her work had helped to make the birthday party a little more special.

When have you worked together with your family? What did you do to help?

Saint Paul's Joy

We are joyful when our family is happy and peaceful. Saint Paul was excited when he heard how some of his friends were growing in their faith. He knew that the more they grew in the love of Jesus Christ, the more they would serve others. He wrote his friends a letter telling them how much he loved them.

I give thanks to God every time I think of you. I pray for you with joy as you help to spread the Gospel. I hold you in my heart. I long to see all of you, and pray that your love and understanding will keep growing. May you continue to make good choices, so you will be pure and blameless when Jesus Christ returns.

adapted from Philippians 1:3–11

Would you like to receive a letter like this? Which words would make you happy?

Did You Know?

Paul was in jail when he wrote this letter. He was put there by people who did not want him to spread Jesus' message. Though he spent many years in jail, his letters were always full of joy.

Our Call to Care

God calls us to care for one another. We start at home with our family. With the grace of the Holy Spirit, we can live together in peace and harmony. We obey and respect our parents, as Jesus did. We treat our family and others with **justice** by treating them fairly.

The Holy Spirit helps us live in peace, harmony, and justice with others. We are to share the Spirit's love with one another. We can help the members of our family. We can help those who cannot help themselves.

My Letter of Thanks

Like Saint Paul, we can tell our families how blessed we are to have them. Think of why you are thankful to belong to your family. Fill in this letter. Tell your family members why they are special to you.

Dear _____,

Thank you for _____

_____

_____

Saint Louise de Marillac Cared

Louise de Marillac lived in France many years ago. When her husband died, she devoted her life to God. She began by visiting poor people and giving them clothes she had sewn and knitted. She met Vincent de Paul, and she helped him care for people who were poor or sick.

Vincent put Louise in charge of a new order of women, the Sisters of Charity. Louise wrote a rule for how these women were to live. Louise decided this religious order would actively serve people in need. She and her community spent their lives working in homes, orphanages, hospitals, and schools. Today, the Sisters of Charity of Saint Vincent de Paul continue to serve those in need all over the world. March 15 is the feast of Saint Louise de Marillac.

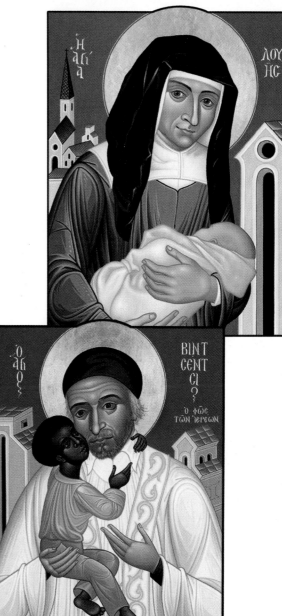

St. Louise de Marillac and
St. Vincent de Paul,
Robert Lentz

Reading God's Word

Bear one another's burdens, and you will fulfill Jesus'
law of love.

adapted from Galatians 6:2

PRAYER

Think of Saint Paul's letter to his friends. He prays for them and holds them in his heart. Close your eyes and picture the members of your family for a moment. Think of how much you love them. Thank God for the gift of your family. Pray that you will continue to grow in love with them.

Now spend a minute talking with Jesus. Tell him the good things you enjoy in your family and parish. Tell Jesus how you will show your love to your family and others you meet. Tell him how you will try especially to help those who cannot help themselves.

Thank Jesus for being with you. Be still and remember Jesus loves you very much. Ask Jesus to bless you and everyone in your family and in your parish.

Faith Summary

Jesus helps us to love and respect one another. Through the grace of God, we can live in peace, harmony, and justice with our families. We share God's love by caring for others, especially those who are poor or elderly.

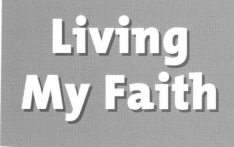

Word I Learned

justice

Ways of Being Like Jesus

We can share God's love by helping others. Offer to do a chore such as shoveling snow, raking leaves, or dropping off mail for a neighbor or relative who needs your help.

With My Family

Jesus obeyed Mary and Joseph. You can be like Jesus by obeying and respecting your parents. If you have brothers or sisters, treat them justly by sharing with them.

PRAYER

Jesus, thank you for showing me how good it is to share your love with others. Help me always to be aware of those who need me so that I can serve others as you did.

My Response

What will you do this week to promote peace and harmony in your home? Draw a picture.

Focus on Faith

Discovering the Holy Spirit in Our Relationships

Through a misunderstanding, a first-grade boy was left alone after school on his first day. He did not know where to go or what to do. As his older sister was leaving school, she realized that her brother might be alone and confused. She went to his classroom, found him, and walked him home. Her care and concern for her brother helped her to respond instinctively to his need for help. Upon reflection, we realize that it is in moments like these that we discover God alive in our family relationships. But these moments do not just happen. They are based on the daily practice of centering our lives on Jesus and following where the Holy Spirit leads us.

Dinnertime Conversation Starter

Has anyone in your family been found when he or she was lost? Share the stories with your child. Assure your child of your constant protection and guidance.

Spirituality in Action

Encourage your child to be obedient to you and respectful to other family members. Strive for peace and harmony in your home. Set a Christian example for your household by being respectful of other people's feelings and needs.

Focus on Prayer

Your child read a letter of Saint Paul in which he tells some of his friends that he will pray for them (Philippians 1:3–11). Encourage your child to pray for family members in a simple way each night, such as by asking God to bless them. Your child can pray especially for family members who are sick or troubled.

Our Catholic Heritage

Your child has read about Saint Louise de Marillac's Sisters of Charity. Her work continues today in the

St. Louise de Marillac, Robert Lentz

United States and Canada in 13 related women's congregations. The Sisters of Charity federation now has about 7,000 members, who share the meaning of God's love through their work worldwide with those who are poor and helpless, and especially those who are elderly. More information is available at **www.sisters-of-charity.org.**

All Life Is Sacred

We witness the beauty of God's creation when we enjoy nature. Where have you seen the beauty of nature? What did you especially enjoy?

PRAYER

Jesus, Son of God, teach me to respect and care for God's wonderful world and all who live in it. I want to be a loving and caring person like you.

A Life of Caring

Every human life is sacred. One person who understood the worth of every person was Blessed Frederic Ozanam.

While Frederic was in college in 1832, a terrible disease broke out in Paris. Many people became sick and died. People who were poor suffered greatly. Each day Frederic would walk past the homes of these families. His parents had raised him to help others. His conscience told him he should help these people.

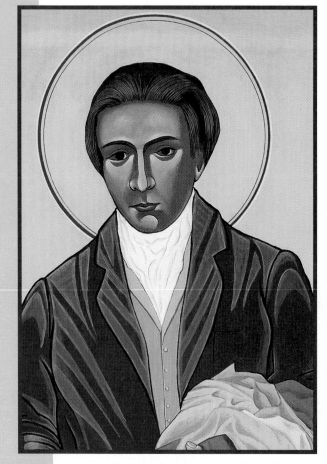

Frederic Ozanam, Fearghal O'Farrell

Six of Frederic's friends decided to help him by giving their wood supply to a widow. Soon they were helping the less fortunate people of Paris in many ways. Some people asked, "How can seven men make a difference?" But they did. They kept working and more people joined them. They called themselves the Society of St. Vincent de Paul after the patron saint of Christian charity. In 1997 Frederic was named Blessed.

Reading God's Word

Let us love one another, because love is from God. Everyone who loves is a child of God and knows God.

adapted from 1 John 4:7

Choosing Respect

Frederic Ozanam knew that every person is special. He knew that all people are important members of the human family. God makes each person sacred from the first moment of life. Like Frederic, we are to treat others with respect, no matter where they are from or what language they speak. God wants people and countries to live peacefully with one another.

Showing Respect by Our Choices

We can show respect for others through the choices we make. God wants us to make choices that are good. Talk about ways you could finish each sentence with a good choice. Take turns making up more sentences.

If I saw two people arguing over a game, I would . . .

If someone made fun of another's clothes, I would . . .

If a friend told me not to be friends with someone, I would . . .

Praise for Our Human Family

God has crowned us with glory and honor. He has asked us to care for his creation: sheep and oxen, the beasts of the field, the birds of the air, and the creatures in the sea.

adapted from Psalm 8:6-10

Parts of Creation

We are called to take care of all of God's creation. A bird, a river, and a friend are all part of God's creation. Think of some parts of creation that begin with the letters below. Write the words on the lines. Use the pictures as hints or make up your own.

C _____ T _____

R _____ I _____

E _____ O _____

A _____ N _____

Small Acts Make a Big Difference

Frederic Ozanam believed God had called him to help others. He did not listen to those who doubted him. He knew that his small acts of kindness could make a big difference.

We can care for God's creation by small acts. We can recycle, clean up our neighborhood, and reuse things instead of throwing them away. We must remember that the world has been given to the whole human family. We must protect the world for those who will come after us.

What is one small thing you can do to keep the world clean and beautiful?

 Link to Liturgy

With the words of the dismissal at Mass, we are sent forth to go in peace and to serve the Lord. Soon we will be ending our year together. We will be sent forth to live what we have learned.

PRAYER

Let us begin today's prayer by remembering what we have learned this year. Think of God as Father. Thank him for the wonderful world he has created for us.

Think of Jesus Christ. Thank him for teaching you about God's love and for showing you how to love God and others.

Think of the Holy Spirit. Thank him for guiding you through the year.

Sit quietly for a moment. Think about how much God loves you. He is with you always. Be still and think of how special you are.

Peacemakers,
Mary Southard, CSJ

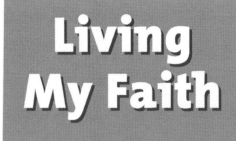
Faith Summary

We are called to treat every person as sacred. God calls us to take care of what he has created. We must care for God's creation today so there will be a beautiful world for the people of the future.

Ways of Being Like Jesus

Jesus cared for sick people. You can be like him by brightening the day of someone who is sick. If someone you know is sick, spend some time with him or her. Do a simple activity or just sit and talk.

With My Family

Talk with your family about how activities such as recycling will help people who will come after us. Find out what things in your home are recycled. Talk about what things can be reused instead of thrown away.

PRAYER

Jesus, thank you for showing me how to respect the world and the people in it. Help me always to live in peace with others.

My Response

What will you do this week to show respect for another person? Will you ask someone about his or her family? Will you invite someone to join in a game? Draw a picture.

RAISING FAITH-FILLED KIDS

a parent page

Frederic Ozanam, Fearghal O'Farrell

Focus on Faith

Blessed Frederic Ozanam Follows Jesus

Blessed Frederic Ozanam (1813–1853) was a Catholic layman in France. In 1832 an epidemic of cholera swept through Paris, killing up to 1,200 people each day. As Frederic walked through the poorer suburbs on his way to the university, he was deeply moved at the hopeless state of families who had lost fathers and mothers. He and six friends decided to see what they could do. They began by giving a widow the remainder of their winter wood supply. Frederic and his friends continued their work. Eventually they formed an association and called it The Society of St. Vincent de Paul. Today the society they began has some 55,000 members in the United States and 1,000,000 worldwide in 130 countries.

Our Catholic Heritage

An example of a program dedicated to helping the poor and vulnerable is sponsored by the National Conference of Bishops of Brazil. This program, called Pastoral da Crianca, or Pastoral of the Child, helps prevent infant deaths and provides nutrition information, medical care, and education to poor families in Brazil. Many School Sisters of Notre Dame are involved in this program, which serves more than a million families a month. It was nominated for a Nobel Peace Prize in 2001.

Dinnertime Conversation Starter

Inquire about the needs of the Society of St. Vincent de Paul nearest your home. The society may even be active in your parish. Discuss how your family can aid the poor by responding to the society's requests.

Spirituality in Action

If you are part of a recycling program, involve your family. Show everyone where to put newspapers, jars, and cans. Explain to your child how he or she can recycle in other ways, such as by reusing bags or wearing hand-me-downs.

Focus on Prayer

Your child has reflected on the beauty of God's creation and the dignity of the human beings to whom God has entrusted its care (Psalm 8:6–10). You may want to read this and other psalms with your child. Remind your child that, by respecting nature and all people, he or she is expressing thanks to God for his creation.

Review

Jesus helps us to make good moral choices and to follow the
Ten Commandments. We are called to practice the virtues of
faith, hope, and charity and to treat all God's creation with
love and respect.

PRAYER

*Jesus, show me how to accept the help you offer me. I want to make
good choices so I can be like you.*

Faith Summary

The virtues of faith, hope, and charity are gifts from God that help us to do good and to live good lives.

Jesus teaches us to make good choices and follow the moral law. The Ten Commandments help us to live for God and others.

Jesus wants us to live in peace, harmony, and justice with our families and with all people. We show the meaning of God's love for us when we love others.

Jesus calls us to care for our world. He wants us to protect the world for those who will come after us.

Learning to Be Like Jesus

We have talked about the many ways Jesus helps us to make good choices. Use the words and ideas you have learned in this unit to fill in this crossword puzzle.

Across

1. When we treat others fairly, we are treating them with _____.

5. When we choose good over evil, we are following the _____ law.

7. God wants us to _____ all his creation.

Down

2. The devil _____ Jesus in the desert, but Jesus kept the first commandment and worshipped God alone.

3. Paul tells us the greatest virtue is _____, or charity.

4. The virtues of faith, _____, and charity help us live a Christian life.

6. Jesus teaches us that all _____ is sacred.

Thumbs Up, Thumbs Down

We have learned ways of making the right moral choice. When we make the right choice, we can give ourselves a "thumbs up." Read each sentence below. If the child is making the right choice, circle the thumbs up. If not, circle the thumbs down. Then talk about the sentences where you circled the thumbs down. What should those children have done to get a thumbs up?

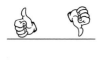

1. Yoko set the table before her mom got home from work.

2. Maria told her friend she was angry and wanted to talk about their problem.

3. Hailey decided not to be friends with Alicia any more because Alicia wouldn't share her snack.

4. Josh spilled juice on his brother's library book by accident and pretended that nothing happened.

5. Seth congratulated Andrew on winning the election even though he had hoped to win himself.

6. Victor waited until his mom left before sneaking a cookie.

PRAYER SERVICE

Leader: *Praise be to God, who fills our lives with love and joy.*

All: *Amen.*

Leader: *In our prayer today, let us praise God in a special way for guiding us and showing us how to live.*

Group A: *Happy are those who live by the teachings of the Lord.*

Group B: *Happy are those who keep God's laws.*

Group A: *They seek the Lord with all their hearts.*

Group B: *They do no wrong.*

All: *They walk in God's ways.*
[adapted from Psalm 119:1–3]

Leader: *Please respond, We praise you, Lord.*

Happy are those who live for God and others.

All: *We praise you, Lord.*

Leader: *Happy are those who live in peace, harmony, and justice.*

All: *We praise you, Lord.*

Leader: *Before we end our time together, let us offer one another a sign of peace.*

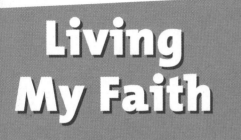

Living My Faith

Ways of Being Like Jesus

Think of three things you would like to do this summer to follow Jesus, such as being kinder to others, sharing with a brother or sister, or fighting less. Ask Jesus for help in meeting these goals.

With My Family

Talk with your family about an activity you can do to keep God's creation beautiful. You can pick up trash at a park in your area or help clean up around your church.

PRAYER

Jesus, my brother, thank you for helping me to make good choices. Support me each day, so I can answer your call to serve others.

My Response

Think of something for which you especially want to thank and praise God. Is it for helping you to make your family a happy one? Is it for helping you to be patient with others? Write a sentence telling God about it.

The Year in Our Church

Lent

Ordinary Time

Christmas

Holy Week

Advent

Ash Wednesday

Epiphany

Palm Sunday
Holy Thursday
Good Friday
Holy Saturday

Christmas

Easter Sunday

Easter

Winter

Spring

First Sunday of Advent

Fall

Summer

All Souls Day
All Saints Day

Ascension
Pentecost

Ordinary Time

Liturgical Calendar

The liturgical calendar shows us the feasts and seasons of the Church year.

Liturgical Year

Advent is the beginning of the Church year and a time of preparation for the birth of Jesus.

Christmas celebrates Jesus' birth. **Epiphany** celebrates Jesus' coming for all people of the world.

Lent is the time for a change of heart, a turning toward God. It prepares us for Easter.

During **Holy Week,** we recall the suffering and death of Jesus.

On **Easter** Sunday, we celebrate Jesus' being raised from the dead. It is a great feast of the Church, a time of hope and joy.

Pentecost celebrates the coming of the Holy Spirit to guide the Church. It ends the Easter season.

All Saints Day celebrates all the holy people who now live with God in heaven.

The time set aside for everyday living of the Christian life is **Ordinary Time.**

Advent

Mary was a young woman who worked hard and prayed often. She loved God and wanted to serve him.

An angel told Mary she was to be the mother of Jesus. Because Mary said yes to God, we can celebrate Jesus' birth.

The Annunciation (detail), Henry Ossawa Tanner, 1898

PRAYER

Dear God, help me this Advent to prepare for Jesus with an open and welcoming heart.

The Angel Visits Mary

God sent the angel Gabriel to a town in Galilee called Nazareth. He was sent to a young woman named Mary, who was engaged to a man named Joseph. The angel said to her, "Hail, favored one! The Lord is with you." Mary was troubled by his words, but he told her not to be afraid. He said, "You will have a son and will name him Jesus. He will be great and will be called Son of the Most High." The angel told her that the child would be holy and people would call him the Son of God.

adapted from Luke 1:26-33

The Annunciation, Henry Ossawa Tanner, 1898

Mary Said Yes to God

Mary trusted God. She said yes when God asked her to be the mother of his Son. She made possible our celebration of Jesus' birth.

As we prepare for Jesus' birth, let us ask Mary to pray for us, so that we too will welcome Jesus into our hearts.

Celebrating Advent With Prayer

During Advent we prepare to welcome Jesus into our hearts. We pray daily as we count the days until Christmas.

My Daily Advent Prayer

Think of some ways you would like to follow Jesus during Advent. Then use your ideas to complete these prayer starters.

Jesus, help me to _____

Jesus, teach me to _____

Jesus, fill me with _____

Jesus, open my heart to _____

Completing Your Prayer

Now use all of your completed prayer starters to compose your own Advent prayer in the space below.

My Advent Prayer

_____

_____

_____

_____

_____

_____

_____

PRAYER SERVICE

Leader: During this holy season of Advent we prepare, as Mary did, for the coming of Jesus. Let us listen to her words and ask her to pray for us.

Reader: A reading from the Gospel of Luke.

The angel Gabriel told Mary she would give birth to a child named Jesus, who would be the Son of God. Mary said, "I am the servant of the Lord. May it be done to me as you have said." Then the angel departed from her. [adapted from Luke 1:35–38]

The gospel of the Lord.

All: Praise to you, Lord Jesus Christ.

Leader: We ask Mary to pray for us.
Holy Mother of God,

All: Pray for us.

Leader: Most honored of women,

All: Pray for us.

Leader: Mary most prayerful,

All: Pray for us.

Leader: Let us close by praying the Hail Mary together.

Nativity—Let the Children Come, Mary Southard, CSJ

On Christmas we celebrate the birth of Jesus. The shepherds heard the angels' message and went to welcome Jesus. As we welcome Jesus, we think about what Jesus' birth means to us.

PRAYER

Jesus, my Savior, show me how to share in your life more fully. I want to share your love with others.

Good News

Mary and Joseph went to Bethlehem to be counted in the census. While they were there, Mary gave birth to Jesus. She put him in a manger because there was no room for them in the inn.

Some shepherds were in a field nearby watching their flock. An angel came to them and told them the good news: "Today in the city of David a savior has been born. He is Messiah and Lord." Then more angels came and said, "Glory to God in the highest."

The shepherds went to Bethlehem, where they found Mary, Joseph, and Jesus. They told Mary and Joseph the angels' message. Mary remembered all these things and kept them in her heart.

Shepherds, Hanna-Cheriyan Varghese

adapted from Luke 2:1-20

Like Mary, we can keep the message of the angels in our hearts. What does the angels' message mean to you?

We Reflect

At Christmas we think about what Jesus' birth means to us. Jesus, the Son of God, became man to share God's life with us. We share in God's life when we love others and treat them fairly.

Symbols of Christmas

There are many symbols of Christmas. The trumpet is a sign of the angels' message to the shepherds. Christmas ornaments remind us of the beauty that Jesus brought into the world. The evergreen tree is a sign of everlasting life.

Think of a symbol of Christmas that you especially enjoy. Draw it in the space below. Talk about how it reminds you of the message of Christmas.

Leader: During this joyful Christmas season, let us praise God.

Group A: Sing to the Lord a new song;

Group B: Sing to the Lord, all the earth.

Group A: Let all the trees of the forest rejoice before the Lord,

Group B: Who comes to rule the world.

Group A: He comes to rule the people

Group B: With justice and truth.

[adapted from Psalm 96:1,12–13]

Leader: We thank God for the gift of his Son.

All: Glory to God in the highest.

Leader: We share the good news as the shepherds did.

All: Glory to God in the highest.

Leader: We share Jesus' love with the world.

All: Glory to God in the highest.

Leader: Let us praise God by praying the Glory Be to the Father.

Lent

Before he began preaching, Jesus wanted to spend time with God. He went to the desert for 40 days to fast and to pray.

We follow Jesus' example during the 40 days of Lent.

 PRAYER

Dear Jesus, help me to keep my Lenten promises. I want to follow your example, so I will be prepared to do what God wants me to do.

Jesus Shows Us the Way

The Holy Spirit led Jesus into the desert to fast and to pray. Jesus stayed there for 40 days. He was tempted by Satan but did not give up his fast. The angels took care of him.

adapted from Mark 1:12-13

The Season of Lent

On Ash Wednesday we receive ashes on our foreheads as a sign of our need for God in our lives. From Ash Wednesday until the Easter Vigil we fast, pray, and share what we have with others. We call this time Lent.

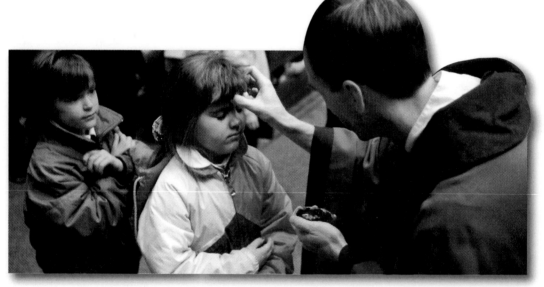

The Holy Spirit guides us during the 40 days of Lent. Just as Jesus was tempted not to obey his Father, we are also tempted not to obey God. God sent the angels to watch over Jesus. God gives us the help we need to live the season of Lent well.

Observing Lent

You can make these 40 days special. You can pray. You can be kind and unselfish. You can be helpful to others. The Holy Spirit will help you do these things every day.

My Lenten CALENDAR

Week 1	Be extra nice to my brother.
Week 2	Do my chores cheerfully.
Week 3	
Week 4	
Week 5	
Week 6	

Lenten Promises

During Lent, we make promises to God. We can promise to give things up, such as a favorite food or television show. We can also promise to do special things, such as praying more often or volunteering at a food pantry. Reminders such as a Lenten Calendar can help us keep our promises.

My Own Lenten Promise

What will you promise to God? Write it on the lines below.

_____

_____

_____

_____

Did You Know?

The ashes we receive on Ash Wednesday are made from the palms blessed the year before on Palm Sunday.

PRAYER SERVICE

Leader: *When Jesus was alone and tempted in the desert, God sent the angels to help him. When we feel lonely and are tempted, God will help us too. Let us listen to Saint Paul's words as he assures his friends that God will be with them.*

Reader: *A reading from the first letter to the Corinthians.*

Your temptations are the same as those of other people. God is faithful. He will not let you be tempted beyond your strength. He will show you a way to overcome temptation. He will make you strong.
[adapted from 1 Corinthians 10:13]

The Word of the Lord.

All: *Thanks be to God.*

Leader: *Let us praise God for giving us the strength we need to keep our Lenten promises.*

All: *Praise to God.*

Holy Week

During Holy Week we remember that Jesus gave his life for us. The Stations of the Cross help us to remember his sacrifice for us.

PRAYER

Jesus, my Savior, show me how to do what is right, even when it is hard. Help me to follow you every day.

Taking Up the Cross

Jesus was put on trial before Pontius Pilate, the Roman governor. Pilate found him to be innocent. Pilate asked the people, "What evil has this man done? I don't think he should be put to death. I will have him whipped and released."

But the people kept shouting for Jesus to be crucified. Finally Pilate handed Jesus over to them to be put to death.

As they led Jesus away, they met a man named Simon of Cyrene. He was coming in from the country. They laid the cross on him and made him carry it behind Jesus.

adapted from Luke 23:22-26

Being Like Simon

Simon of Cyrene helped Jesus to carry the cross. We can help Jesus too. Like Simon, we are called to do what is right in our lives, even if it is hard. We can comfort someone who is sad. We can help at home without complaining. Jesus said that when we do something to help someone else, we do it for him.

Stations of the Cross

After Jesus' death and resurrection, early Christians visited Jerusalem, the city where Jesus died, to walk in his footsteps. They stopped at different places along the way to remember what happened to Jesus. They marked the places where they stopped so others could follow. These places became the Stations of the Cross.

Like the early Christians, we can pray the Stations of the Cross to remember all that Jesus did for us. At each station we stop, pray quietly, and thank Jesus for his great sacrifice.

A Message to Jesus

Imagine you are in the crowd as Jesus carries his cross. Write what you would say to Jesus.

Jesus, _____

_____

_____

_____

_____

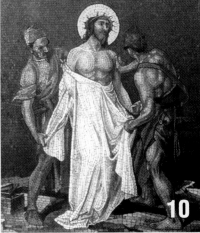

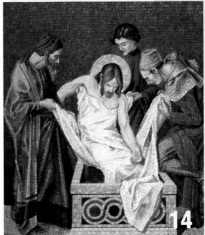

PRAYER SERVICE

Leader: *Just as Simon helped Jesus, we can help lighten the burdens of others. Let us listen to what Jesus tells us.*

Reader: *A reading from the Gospel of Luke.*

Jesus said to all the people, "If any of you want to follow me, you must not think about yourself. You must take up your cross each day and follow me."

[adapted from Luke 9:23]

The gospel of the Lord.

All: *Praise to you, Lord Jesus Christ.*

Leader: *We ask Jesus to help us take up our daily crosses. We ask him to give us the grace to help others bear their crosses.*

We adore you, O Lord Jesus Christ, and we bless your holy name.

All: *Because by your holy cross, you have redeemed the world.*

Easter

Jesus' friends were very sad. Their best friend had died. When they went to anoint his body one last time, they were surprised to find the tomb empty. Jesus had risen from the dead!

On Easter we remember this special day. We celebrate the Resurrection of Jesus. We share in the joy that Jesus' friends felt.

He Is Risen, He Qi, 1998

 PRAYER

Jesus, risen Lord, help me remember that you died and rose for me. I want to celebrate the miracle of your Resurrection by serving God and others.

Jesus was probably buried in a tomb like this.

Jesus Is Alive!

It was dawn on the first day of the week. Jesus' friend Mary Magdalene and several other women went to his tomb to serve him one last time. They brought spices to anoint his body. They found the tomb empty. Then two men in beautiful clothes came to them. The men said, "Why are you looking for Jesus among the dead? He is not here. He has been raised from the dead. Remember that Jesus told you he would rise on the third day." Upon hearing this, the women remembered Jesus' words.

adapted from Luke 24:1-8

The News Spreads

After he rose, Jesus appeared to Mary Magdalene and the other women. He appeared to Peter, to the disciples, and to many more people. After some time, Jesus returned to his Father, where he lives today. We will someday be happy with Jesus in heaven.

The Lord's Day

We remember that Jesus was raised to new life on Sunday, the Lord's day. On this day we celebrate Jesus' living presence, especially in the Eucharist. Meeting Jesus in the Eucharist is important. The Church asks us to receive Jesus in Holy Communion often.

An Easter Message

After they found the tomb empty, Mary Magdalene and the other women told the disciples what they had seen and heard. We repeat their message on Easter. Imagine you have a friend who does not understand why you celebrate Easter. In the spaces below, share the Easter message with your friend.

Friend: What happened on Easter?

You: _____

_____

_____

Friend: Why is Easter so important?

You: _____

_____

_____

Friend: What do you do to celebrate Easter?

You: _____

_____

_____

PRAYER SERVICE

Leader: As believers in Jesus' Resurrection, we want to share the good news of Easter with others. Saint Paul wants his friends to share in the joy of Jesus' Resurrection. Let us listen to his words.

Reader: A reading from the first letter to the Corinthians.

My friends, I want to remind you of the message I gave you that you believed. Through it, you are being saved. Jesus died for our sins. He was buried and was raised on the third day. All this was in keeping with the Scriptures. [adapted from 1 Corinthians 15:1–4]

The Word of the Lord.

All: Thanks be to God.

Leader: Let us close by proclaiming the mystery of our faith.

All: Dying you destroyed our death, rising you restored our life. Lord Jesus, come in glory. Amen. Alleluia.

Pentecost

On Pentecost we celebrate the gift of the Holy Spirit.
The Holy Spirit strengthens us to continue Jesus' mission.

 PRAYER

*Dear Jesus, help me to use my special gifts. I want to live as your
disciple and continue your work.*

One in the Spirit

Paul wanted his friends in Corinth to understand how the Holy Spirit works in each of us. He sent them this message.

> There are different gifts, but one Spirit. The same God works in all of us. The Spirit gives each of us a different way to serve. If the Holy Spirit is in you, you will say, "Jesus is Lord."
>
> We are all different. We may be Jews or Greeks, enslaved or free persons. When we were baptized in one Spirit, we all became part of the one body of Christ. The same Spirit helps us all.

adapted from 1 Corinthians 12:3b-7,12-13

Paul tells us that each of us has special gifts. The Holy Spirit helps us use these gifts. What are your gifts? How do you use them?

Did You Know?

The word *Pentecost* comes from a Greek word that means 50. Pentecost is seven weeks, or 50 days, after Easter.

Finish the Story

Finish the Story

In this story, the gifts of many people help make the church play a success. Finish the story by filling in the gifts listed below.

kindness   singing   creativity   dance   joy   patience

The Big Night

Backstage, the third graders were warming

up for the church play. Marcos cleared his

throat and practiced his _____.

Maria put on her shoes and practiced her

_____ steps. Everybody was

filled with _____.

Months of hard work were paying off.

So much had gone into this play. It took the

_____ of Jose and Lisa to create the

beautiful scenery. It took the _____ of the

local store manager, who gave the cast beautiful costumes to

wear. If it weren't for the _____ of their

director, Mr. Kessell, the third graders might never have learned

their lines. Thanks to the gifts they all shared, they knew the

church play would be a success.

PRAYER SERVICE

Leader: *Praise be to God, who fills our lives with love and joy.*

All: *Amen.*

Leader: *Jesus kept his promise to send the Spirit to be with us. Let us pray that we will live according to the Spirit.*

All: *Amen.*

Reader: *A reading from the Gospel of John.*

I will ask the Father to send you a helper. The Holy Spirit will come to you. He will stay with you always. I will not leave you orphans. I will come to you.

[adapted from John 14:16–18]

The gospel of the Lord.

All: *Praise to you, Lord Jesus Christ.*

Leader: *Jesus, thank you for being with us.*

All: *Make us one with you and with one another.
Amen.*

All Saints Day

Painting on cloth depicting Ethiopian saints (detail)

On the feast of All Saints we remember those who have died and are with God in heaven. We can ask the saints to pray to God for us today and every day. This prayer will help us to follow the good example of their lives.

PRAYER

Jesus, help me to love and serve others as you did. I want to be united with you and others.

Loving One Another

We become holy like the saints when we serve others as Jesus did. Jesus wants us to be kind to one another at school, at home, and wherever we are. Through the sacraments, the Holy Spirit gives us the grace we need to love one another. In the New Testament, Saint John tells us that God's love grows in us when we love one another.

John says, "Friends, because God loves us so much, we also must love one another. If we love one another, God remains in us, and his love grows in us. This is how we know that we remain in him and he in us. God has given us his Spirit."

adapted from 1 John 4:11-13

The Communion of Saints

We are not alone! We are united with all those who love God, both living and dead. This is called the Communion of Saints. We are to pray for one another and for those who have died.

Saints in Heaven and on Earth

We celebrate the feast of All Saints on November 1. We remember all those who have died and are enjoying life with God in heaven. We remember that as followers of Jesus on earth, we are all united in Jesus Christ.

A Saint in the Making

We are living like the saints when we help others. Draw a picture of yourself in the frame below. On the lines, write phrases describing what you can do to follow the example of the saints.

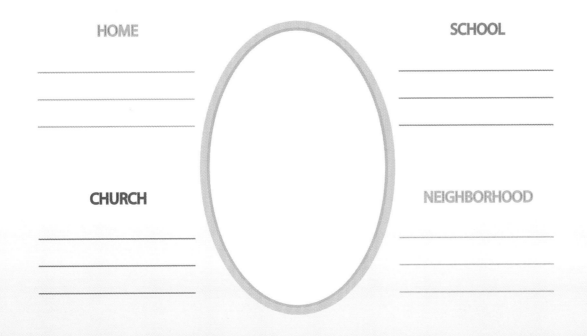

HOME

SCHOOL

CHURCH

NEIGHBORHOOD

PRAYER SERVICE

Leader: Let us praise our loving God. Blessed be God for ever.

All: Blessed be God for ever.

Leader: Jesus is our example of God's love for us.
We pray that in everything we do we will follow
him and become holy.

Reader: A reading from the first letter to the Corinthians.

A body is one, even though it has many parts.
We were all baptized into the one body of Christ.
We are one in the Spirit.

[adapted from 1 Corinthians 12:12–13]

The Word of the Lord.

All: Thanks be to God.

Leader: We ask the saints in heaven to pray to God
for us. Let us close with our special prayer in
which we ask Mary to pray for us.

Prayers and Practices of Our Faith

Grade 3

Knowing and Praying Our Faith

I am aware of God's love when I listen to the ocean.

233

Celebrating Our Faith

Living Our Faith

Songs of Our Faith

Understanding the Words of Our Faith

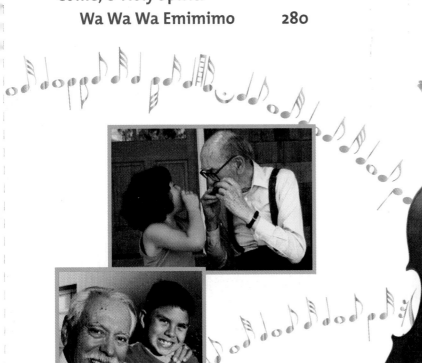

The Bible and You

God speaks to us in many ways. One way is through the Bible. The Bible is the story of God's promise to care for us, especially through his Son, Jesus.

The Bible is made up of two parts. The Old Testament tells stories about the Jewish people before Jesus was born.

A beautiful part of the Old Testament is the Book of Psalms. A psalm is a prayer in the form of a poem. There are 150 psalms.

The New Testament tells stories about Jesus' life, death, and resurrection. In the New Testament, Jesus teaches us about the Father's love.

Copyists in Wales are now working on the Saint John's Bible, the first handwritten, illuminated Bible in the modern era.

In the Gospels, Jesus taught, using parables. A parable is a simple story Jesus told to show us what God wants for the world. The story of the Good Samaritan is an example of a parable.

At Mass we hear stories from the Bible. We can also read the Bible on our own.

Prayer and How We Pray

Prayer is talking and listening to God. When we pray, we raise our hearts and minds to God. We can talk to God in the special words of prayers or in our own words. We can pray aloud or quietly in our hearts.

We can pray to God often and in many different ways. We can praise God. We can ask God for what we need and thank him for what we have. We can pray for ourselves and for others.

Prayers to Take to Heart

It is good for us to know prayers by heart. To learn prayers by heart means that we not only learn, or memorize, the words but also try to understand and live them.

Sign of the Cross

In the name of the Father,
and of the Son,
and of the Holy Spirit.
Amen.

Lord's Prayer

Our Father,
who art in heaven,
hallowed be thy name;
thy kingdom come;
thy will be done
on earth as it is in heaven.
Give us this day our daily bread;
and forgive us our trespasses
as we forgive those who trespass
against us; and lead us not into temptation,
but deliver us from evil. Amen.

Hail Mary

Hail Mary, full of grace,
the Lord is with you.
Blessed are you among women,
and blessed is the fruit of your womb, Jesus.
Holy Mary, Mother of God,
pray for us sinners,
now and at the hour of our death.
Amen.

Glory Be to the Father

Glory be to the Father,
and to the Son,
and to the Holy Spirit.
As it was in the beginning,
is now, and ever shall be,
world without end.
Amen.

Prayer Before Meals

Bless us, O Lord, and these your gifts
which we are about to receive from your goodness.
Through Christ our Lord.
Amen.

Prayer After Meals

We give you thanks
for all your gifts,
almighty God,
living and reigning
now and for ever.
Amen.

Act of Contrition

My God,

I am sorry for my sins with all my heart.

In choosing to do wrong

and failing to do good,

I have sinned against you

whom I should love above all things.

I firmly intend, with your help,

to do penance,

to sin no more,

and to avoid whatever leads me to sin.

Our Savior Jesus Christ

suffered and died for us.

In his name, my God, have mercy.

Prayer to the Holy Spirit

Come, Holy Spirit, fill the hearts
  of your faithful.
And kindle in them the fire
  of your love.
Send forth your Spirit and
  they shall be created.
And you will renew the face of the earth.

Lord,
by the light of the Holy Spirit
you have taught the hearts of your faithful.
In the same Spirit
help us to relish what is right
and always rejoice in your consolation.
We ask this through Christ our Lord.
Amen.

Morning Offering

My God, I offer you my prayers,
works, joys and sufferings of this day
in union with the holy sacrifice of the Mass throughout the world.
I offer them for all the intentions of your Son's Sacred Heart,
for the salvation of souls, reparation for sin,
and the reunion of Christians.
Amen.

Apostles' Creed

I believe in God, the Father almighty,
  creator of heaven and earth.
I believe in Jesus Christ, his only Son, our Lord.
  He was conceived by the power of the Holy Spirit
    and born of the Virgin Mary.
  He suffered under Pontius Pilate,
    was crucified, died, and was buried.
  He descended to the dead.
  On the third day he arose again.
  He ascended into heaven,
    and is seated at the right hand of the Father.
  He will come again to judge the living and the dead.
I believe in the Holy Spirit,
  the holy catholic Church,
  the communion of saints,
  the forgiveness of sins,
  the resurrection of the body,
  and the life everlasting. Amen.

Hail, Holy Queen

Hail, holy Queen, Mother of mercy,
hail, our life, our sweetness, and our hope.
To you we cry, the children of Eve;
to you we send up our sighs,
mourning and weeping in this land of exile.
Turn, then, most gracious advocate,
your eyes of mercy toward us;
lead us home at last
and show us the blessed fruit of your womb, Jesus:
O clement, O loving, O sweet Virgin Mary.

Prayer for Vocations

God, thank you for loving me.
In Baptism you called me by name
to live as your child.
Help all your people to know their call in life.
For your greater glory, raise up generous leaders
to serve as priests, deacons, sisters, and brothers.
Amen.

The Rosary

The Rosary helps us to pray to Jesus through Mary. When we pray the Rosary, we think about the special events, or mysteries, in the lives of Jesus and Mary.

A rosary is made up of a string of beads and a crucifix. We hold the crucifix in our hands as we pray the Sign of the Cross. Then we pray the Apostles' Creed.

Between the crucifix and the medal of Mary, there is a single bead, followed by a set of three beads and another single bead. We pray the Lord's Prayer as we hold the first single bead and a Hail Mary at each bead in the set of three that follows. Then we pray the Glory Be to the Father. On the next single bead we think about the first mystery and pray the Lord's Prayer.

There are five sets of ten beads; each set is called a decade. We pray a Hail Mary on each bead of a decade as we reflect on a particular mystery in the lives of Jesus and Mary. The Glory Be to the Father is prayed at the end of each decade. Between decades is a single bead on which we think about one of the mysteries and pray the Lord's Prayer.

We end by holding the crucifix in our hands as we pray the Sign of the Cross.

Praying the Rosary

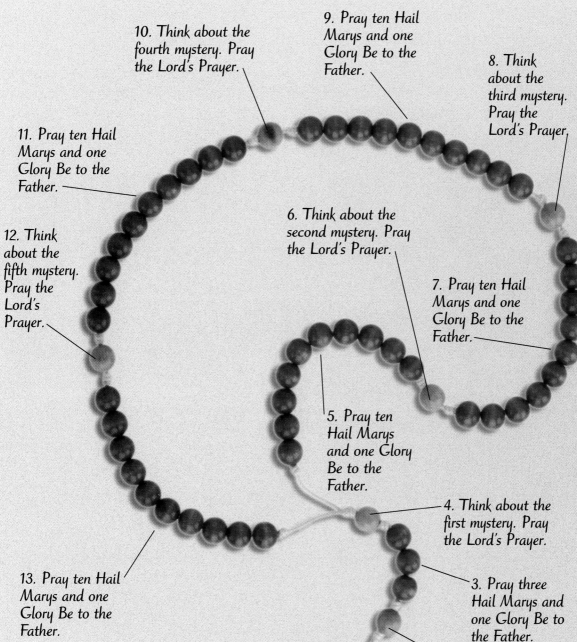

10. Think about the fourth mystery. Pray the Lord's Prayer.

9. Pray ten Hail Marys and one Glory Be to the Father.

8. Think about the third mystery. Pray the Lord's Prayer.

11. Pray ten Hail Marys and one Glory Be to the Father.

6. Think about the second mystery. Pray the Lord's Prayer.

12. Think about the fifth mystery. Pray the Lord's Prayer.

7. Pray ten Hail Marys and one Glory Be to the Father.

5. Pray ten Hail Marys and one Glory Be to the Father.

4. Think about the first mystery. Pray the Lord's Prayer.

13. Pray ten Hail Marys and one Glory Be to the Father.

3. Pray three Hail Marys and one Glory Be to the Father.

2. Pray the Lord's Prayer.

14. Pray the Sign of the Cross.

1. Pray the Sign of the Cross and the Apostles' Creed.

Mysteries of the Rosary

The Church has used three sets of mysteries for many years. In 2002 Pope John Paul II proposed a fourth set of mysteries—the Mysteries of Light, or Luminous Mysteries. According to his suggestion, the four sets of mysteries might be prayed on the following days: the Joyful Mysteries on Monday and Saturday, the Sorrowful Mysteries on Tuesday and Friday, the Glorious Mysteries on Wednesday and Sunday, and the Luminous Mysteries on Thursday.

The Joyful Mysteries

1. *The Annunciation*   Mary learns she has been chosen to be the mother of Jesus.

2. *The Visitation*   Mary visits Elizabeth, who tells Mary that she will always be remembered.

3. *The Nativity*   Jesus is born in a stable in Bethlehem.

4. *The Presentation*   Mary and Joseph take the infant Jesus to the Temple to present him to God.

5. *The Finding of Jesus in the Temple*   Jesus is found in the Temple, discussing his faith with the teachers.

The Mysteries of Light

1. *The Baptism of Jesus in the River Jordan*   God proclaims Jesus is his beloved Son.

2. *The Wedding Feast at Cana*   At Mary's request, Jesus performs his first miracle.

3. *The Proclamation of the Kingdom of God*   Jesus calls all to conversion and service to the Kingdom of God.

4. *The Transfiguration of Jesus*   Jesus is revealed in glory to Peter, James, and John.

5. *The Institution of the Eucharist*   Jesus offers his Body and Blood at the Last Supper.

The Sorrowful Mysteries

1. *The Agony in the Garden*
   Jesus prays in the Garden
   of Gethsemane on the night
   before he dies.

2. *The Scourging at the Pillar*
   Jesus is beaten with whips.

3. *The Crowning With Thorns*
   Jesus is mocked and crowned
   with thorns.

4. *The Carrying of the Cross*
   Jesus carries the cross on which he will be crucified.

5. *The Crucifixion*   Jesus is nailed to the cross and dies.

The Glorious Mysteries

1. *The Resurrection*   God the
   Father raises Jesus from
   the dead.

2. *The Ascension*   Jesus returns to
   his Father in heaven.

3. *The Coming of the Holy Spirit*
   The Holy Spirit comes to bring
   new life to the disciples.

4. *The Assumption of Mary*   At the
   end of her life on earth, Mary is
   taken body and soul into heaven.

5. *The Coronation of Mary*   Mary is
   crowned as Queen of heaven and
   earth.

Stations of the Cross

The fourteen Stations of the Cross represent events from Jesus' passion and death. At each station we use our senses and our imagination to reflect prayerfully on Jesus' suffering, death, and resurrection.

1. Jesus Is Condemned to Death.
Pontius Pilate condemns Jesus to death.

2. Jesus Takes Up His Cross.
Jesus willingly accepts and patiently bears his cross.

3. Jesus Falls the First Time.
Weakened by torments and by loss of blood, Jesus falls beneath his cross.

4. Jesus Meets His Sorrowful Mother.
Jesus meets his mother, Mary, who is filled with grief.

5. Simon of Cyrene Helps Jesus Carry the Cross.
Soldiers force Simon of Cyrene to carry the cross.

6. Veronica Wipes the Face of Jesus.
Veronica steps through the crowd to wipe the face of Jesus.

7. Jesus Falls a Second Time.
Jesus falls beneath the weight of the cross a second time.

8. Jesus Meets the Women of Jerusalem.
Jesus tells the women to weep not for him but for themselves and for their children.

9. Jesus Falls the Third Time.
Weakened almost to the point of death, Jesus falls a third time.

10. Jesus Is Stripped of His Garments.
The soldiers strip Jesus of his garments, treating him as a common criminal.

11. Jesus Is Nailed to the Cross.
Jesus' hands and feet are nailed to the cross.

12. Jesus Dies on the Cross.
After suffering greatly on the cross, Jesus bows his head and dies.

13. Jesus Is Taken Down From the Cross.
The lifeless body of Jesus is tenderly placed in the arms of Mary, his mother.

14. Jesus Is Laid in the Tomb.
Jesus' disciples place his body in the tomb.

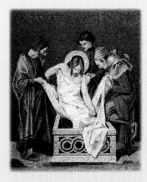

The closing prayer—sometimes included as a fifteenth station—reflects on the Resurrection of Jesus.

The Seven Sacraments, window made by students of Saint Malachy School, Burlington, Mass.

The Seven Sacraments

The sacraments are signs of the grace we receive from God.

Sacraments show that God is part of our lives. They were given to the Church by Jesus. They help us to live the way God wants us to live. The sacraments are celebrated with us by priests.

Sacraments of Initiation

These sacraments lay the foundation of every Christian life.

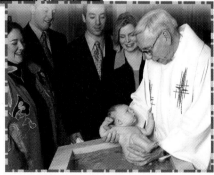

Baptism

Baptism is the first sacrament we receive. Through Baptism we become followers of Jesus and part of God's family, the Church. The pouring of water is the main sign of Baptism.

Confirmation

In this sacrament the Holy Spirit strengthens us to be witnesses to Jesus. Confirmation seals our life of faith in Jesus and helps us become better Christians.

The bishop places holy oil on our foreheads in the form of a cross. This is the main sign of Confirmation.

Eucharist

At Mass the bread and wine become Jesus' Body and Blood. This happens when the priest says the words of consecration that Jesus used at the Last Supper. The Eucharist is also called Holy Communion.

Sacraments of Healing

These sacraments celebrate the healing power of Jesus.

Penance

We ask God to forgive our sins in the Sacrament of Penance. The priest who celebrates this sacrament with us shares Jesus' gifts of peace and forgiveness.

The Holy Spirit helps us to be sorry for our sins. God always forgives us when we are sorry and do penance for our sins.

Anointing of the Sick

In this sacrament a sick person is anointed with holy oil and receives the spiritual—and sometimes even the physical—healing of Jesus.

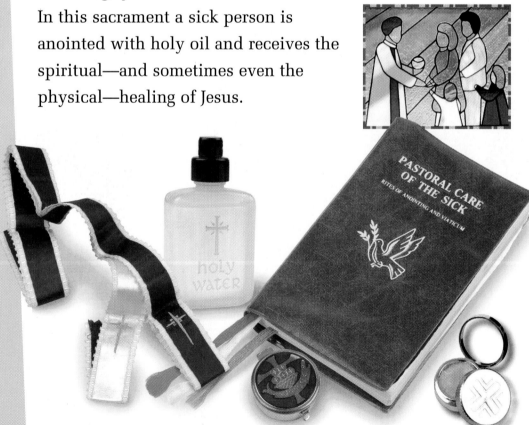

Sacraments at the Service of Communion

These sacraments help members serve the community.

Holy Orders

Some men are called to be deacons, priests, or bishops. They receive the Sacrament of Holy Orders. Through Holy Orders the mission, or task, given by Jesus to his apostles continues in the Church.

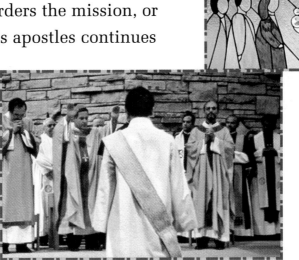

Matrimony

Some men and women are called by the Holy Spirit to be married. They agree to live in faithful love in the Sacrament of Matrimony.

They make a solemn promise to be partners for life, both for their own good and for the good of the children they will raise.

Celebrating the Lord's Day

Sunday is the day on which we celebrate the Resurrection of Jesus. It is the Lord's day. We gather for Mass and rest from work. People all over the world gather at God's eucharistic table as brothers and sisters.

Order of the Mass

The Mass is the high point of the Christian life, and it always follows a set order.

Introductory Rite—preparing to celebrate the Eucharist

Entrance Procession
We gather as a community and praise God in song.

Sign of the Cross and Greeting
We pray the Sign of the Cross. The priest welcomes us.

Penitential Rite
We remember our sins and ask God for mercy.

Gloria
We praise God in song.

Opening Prayer
We ask God to hear our prayers.

Liturgy of the Word—hearing God's plan
of salvation

First Reading

We listen to God's Word, usually from the
Old Testament.

Responsorial Psalm

We respond to God's Word in song.

Second Reading

We listen to God's Word from the New Testament.

Alleluia or Gospel Acclamation

We sing "Alleluia!" (except during Lent) to praise
God for his Word.

Gospel

We stand and listen to the gospel of the Lord.

Homily

The priest or the deacon explains God's Word.

Profession of Faith

We proclaim our faith through the Creed.

General Intercessions

We pray for our needs and the needs of others.

Liturgy of the Eucharist—celebrating Jesus' presence in the Eucharist

Preparation of the Altar and the Gifts

We bring gifts of bread and wine to the altar.

- Prayer Over the Gifts—The priest prays that God will accept our sacrifice.

Eucharistic Prayer

This prayer of thanksgiving is the center and high point of the entire celebration.

- Preface—We give thanks and praise to God.

- Holy, Holy—We sing an acclamation of praise.

- Consecration—The bread and wine become the Body and Blood of Jesus Christ.

- Memorial Acclamation—We proclaim the mystery of our faith.

- Great Amen—We affirm the words and actions of the eucharistic prayer.

Communion Rite

We prepare to receive the Body and Blood of Jesus Christ.

- Lord's Prayer—We pray the Our Father.

- Sign of Peace—We offer one another Christ's peace.

- Breaking of the Bread and the Lamb of God— We pray for forgiveness, mercy, and peace.

- Communion—We receive the Body and Blood of Jesus Christ.

- Prayer After Communion— We pray that the Eucharist will strengthen us to live as Jesus did.

Concluding Rite—going forth to serve the
Lord and others

Blessing
We receive God's blessing.

Dismissal
We go in peace to love and serve the Lord
and one another.

Receiving Communion

When we go to communion, we receive the Body of Christ—in the
form of bread—in our hands or on our tongues. The priest or the
eucharistic minister says, "The Body of Christ." We reply, "Amen."

We can also receive the Blood of Christ in the form of wine. The
priest or the minister offers us the cup and says, "The Blood of
Christ." We reply, "Amen." We take the cup in our hands and
drink from it; we then hand it back to the priest or the minister.

Holy Days of Obligation

Holy Days of Obligation are the days other than Sundays on
which we celebrate the great things God has done for us
through Jesus and the saints. On Holy Days of Obligation,
Catholics gather for Mass.

Six Holy Days of Obligation are celebrated in the United States.

January 1—Mary, Mother of God
Forty days after Easter—Ascension
August 15—Assumption of the Blessed Virgin Mary
November 1—All Saints
December 8—Immaculate Conception
December 25—Nativity of Our Lord Jesus Christ

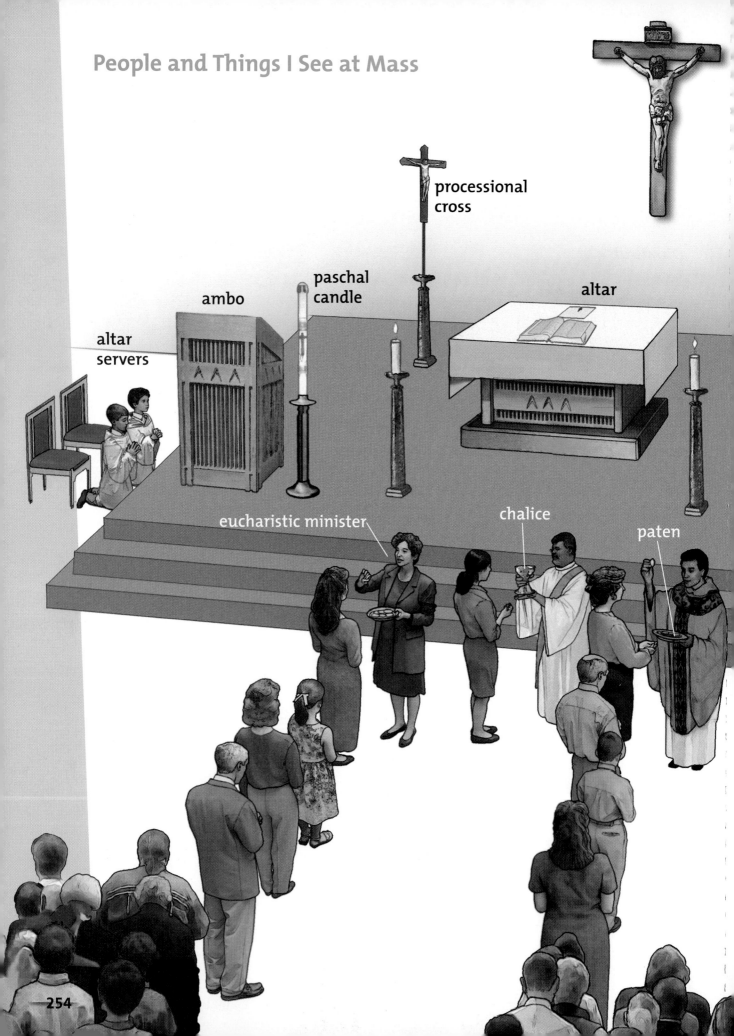

People and Things I See at Mass

processional cross

paschal candle

ambo

altar

altar servers

eucharistic minister

chalice

paten

254

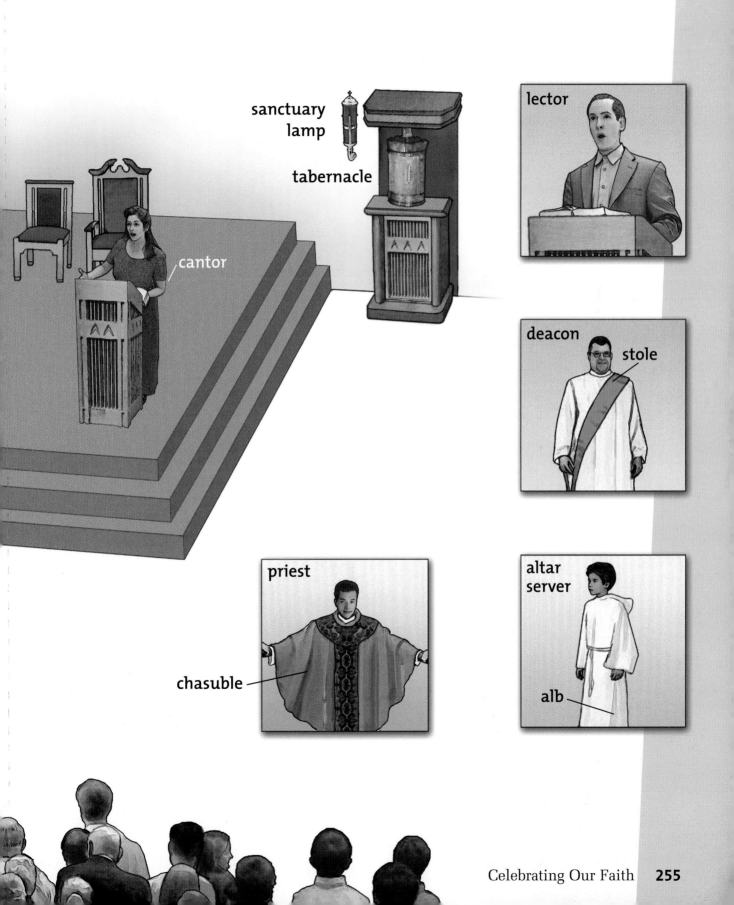

sanctuary lamp

tabernacle

cantor

lector

deacon

stole

priest

chasuble

altar server

alb

An Examination of Conscience

An examination of conscience is the act of reflecting on how we have hurt our relationships with God and others. Questions such as the following will help us in our examination of conscience:

My Relationship With God

Do I use God's name with love and reverence?
What steps am I taking to grow closer to God and to others?

Do I actively participate at Mass on Sundays and holy days?
Do I pray?

Am I willing to turn to God often, especially when I am tempted?

My Relationships With Family, Friends, and Neighbors

Have I set a bad example by my words or actions? Do I treat others fairly? Do I spread stories that hurt other people?

Am I loving to those in my family? Am I respectful of my neighbors, my friends, and those in authority?

Do I show respect for my body and for the bodies of others?

Have I taken or damaged anything that did not belong to me? Have I cheated, copied homework, or lied?

Do I quarrel or fight with others? Do I try to hurt people who I think have hurt me?

How to Go to Confession

An examination of conscience is an important part of preparing for the Sacrament of Penance. The Sacrament of Penance includes the following steps:

1. The priest greets us and we pray the Sign of the Cross. He invites us to trust in God. He may read God's Word with us.

2. We confess our sins. The priest may help and counsel us.

3. The priest gives us a penance to perform. Penance can be an act of kindness or prayers to pray, or both.

4. The priest asks us to express our sorrow, usually by praying the Act of Contrition.

5. We receive absolution. The priest says, "I absolve you from your sins in the name of the Father, and of the Son, and of the Holy Spirit." We respond, "Amen."

6. The priest dismisses us by saying, "Go in peace." We go forth to perform the act of penance he has given us.

The Ten Commandments

God gave us the Ten Commandments. They teach us how to live for God and for others. They help us follow the moral law to do good and avoid evil.

1. I am your God; love nothing more than me.

2. Use God's name with respect.

3. Keep the Lord's day holy.

4. Honor and obey your parents.

5. Treat all human life with respect.

6. Respect married life.

7. Respect what belongs to others.

8. Tell the truth.

9. Respect your neighbors and your friends.

10. Be happy with what you have.

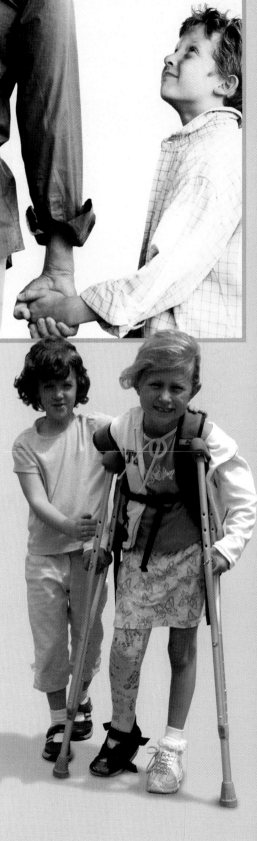

The Great Commandment

People asked Jesus, "What is the most important commandment?" Jesus said, "First, love God. Love him with your heart, soul, and mind. The second is like it: Love your neighbor as much as you love yourself."

adapted from Matthew 22:37–39

We call this the Great Commandment.

The New Commandment

Before his death on the cross, Jesus gave his disciples a new commandment: "Love one another. As I have loved you, so you also should love one another." (*John 13:34*)

The Beatitudes

Jesus gave us the Beatitudes in the Sermon on the Mount. They show us the way to true happiness.

Blessed are those who need God.
They will live in heaven one day.

Blessed are those who are sad.
They will be comforted.

Blessed are those who have little.
They will be given many things.

Blessed are those who have mercy on others.
They will be shown mercy.

Blessed are those who make peace.
They are the children of God.

adapted from Matthew 5:1–10

The Beatitudes, Jesus Mafa

Making Good Choices

The Holy Spirit helps us to make good choices. We get help from the Ten Commandments, the grace of the sacraments, and the teachings of the Church. We also get help from the example of saints and fellow Christians. To make good choices, we ask the following questions:

1. Is the thing I'm choosing to do a good thing?

2. Am I choosing to do it for the right reasons?

3. Am I choosing to do it at the right time and place?

Fruits of the Holy Spirit

When we realize that the Holy Spirit lives within us, we live the way God wants us to. The Fruits of the Holy Spirit are signs of the Holy Spirit's action in our lives.

love	**joy**	**peace**
patience	**kindness**	**generosity**
faithfulness	**gentleness**	**self-control**

Church Tradition also includes **goodness, modesty,** and **chastity** as Fruits of the Holy Spirit.

Showing Our Love for the World

Jesus taught us to care for those in need. The social teachings of the Church call for us to follow Jesus' example in each of the following areas:

Life and Dignity

God wants us to care for everyone. We are all made in his image.

Family and Community

Jesus wants us to be loving helpers in our families and communities.

Rights and Responsibilities

All people should have what they need to live good lives.

The Poor and Vulnerable

Jesus calls us to do what we can to help people in need.

Work and Workers

The work that we do gives glory to God.

Solidarity

Since God is our Father, we are called to treat everyone in the world as a brother or a sister.

God's Creation

We show our love for God's world by taking care of it.

Song of Love

Chorus

Thank you Je - sus for help - ing me to see.

Thank you God for the heart you've giv - en me.

Thank you Spir - it for com - ing to me, and for show - ing me how to sing

your song of love.

(to Verse 1)

your song of love.

(to Verses 2 and 3)

your song of love.

(Fine)

Verse 1

I saw some - one lone - ly by the road,

Some - one my age sad - ly all a - lone.

I shared my friend - ship and we talked a while.

(to Chorus)

I gave a hand, Je - sus gave back a smile.

continued

Song of Love (continued)

Verse 2

Bm   G   A   D

I saw Je - sus in - side my heart.

Em   A   G   D

Mak - ing me God's own work of art

Bm   G   A   D

If I spread my joy in life each day

Em   A   G   A   D

I can show my love for God's world in ev - 'ry way.

Verse 3

Bm · G · A · D

I saw Je - sus in friends and fam - i - ly

Em · A · G · D

By my side, shar - ing and sup - port - ing me.

Bm · G · A · D

I found my heart had room for ev - 'ry - one.

Em · A · G A D · (to Chorus)

Thank you Spir - it for what you have be - gun.

"Song of Love" lyrics by E. Strauss; music by Neilson Hubbard.
Copyright © 2004 by Loyola Press. All rights reserved.

Here I Am, God

Refrain

C   F

Here   I   am,   God.   I   am   com - ing.

C   G

My   de - light   is   to   do   your   will!

C   F

Here   I   am,   God.   I   am   com - ing.

C   G   C

My   de - light   is   to   do   your   will.

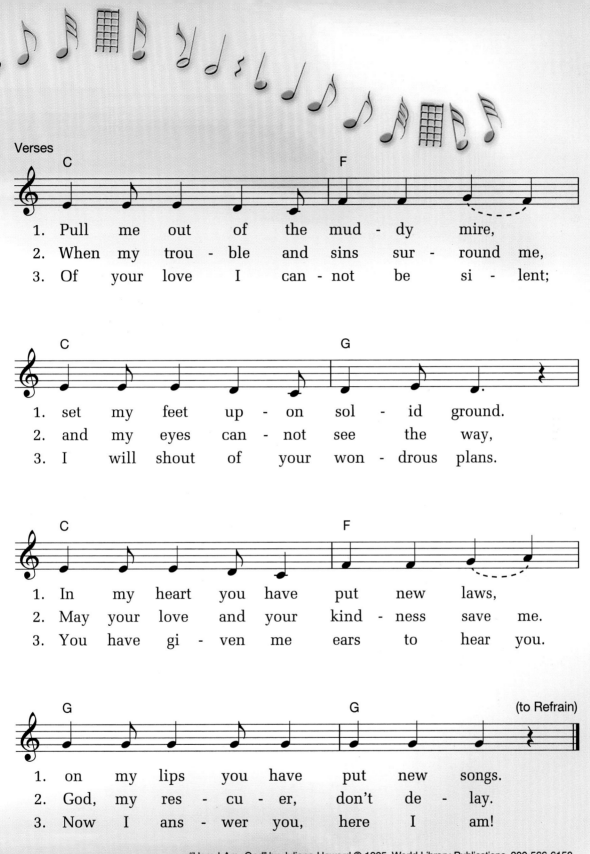

Verses

C   F

1. Pull me out of the mud - dy mire,
2. When my trou - ble and sins sur - round me,
3. Of your love I can - not be si - lent;

C   G

1. set my feet up - on sol - id ground.
2. and my eyes can - not see the way,
3. I will shout of your won - drous plans.

C   F

1. In my heart you have put new laws,
2. May your love and your kind - ness save me.
3. You have gi - ven me ears to hear you.

G   G   (to Refrain)

1. on my lips you have put new songs.
2. God, my res - cu - er, don't de - lay.
3. Now I ans - wer you, here I am!

Holy Is Your Name

Refrain

And ho - ly is your name through all gen - er-

a - tions! E - ver - last - ing is your mer - cy to the

peo - ple you have cho - sen, and ho - ly is your name.

Verses

G

1. My soul is filled with joy as I
2. I am low - ly as a child, but I
3. In your love you now ful - fill what you

C   Em

1. sing to God my sav - ior: you have looked u - pon your
2. know from this day for - ward that my name will be re -
3. pro - mised to your peo - ple. I will praise you, Lord, my

Am

1. ser - vant, you have vis - it - ed your
2. mem - bered, for all will call me
3. sav - ior, e - ver - last - ing is your

G   (to Refrain)

1. peo - ple, and ho - ly is your name.
2. bless - ed, and ho - ly is your name.
3. mer - cy, and ho - ly is your name.

I Say "Yes," Lord / Digo "Sí," Señor

1. I say "Yes," my Lord, in
2. *Di - go "Sí," Se - ñor, en*

1. all the good times, through all the bad times,
2. *tiem - pos mal - os, en tiem - pos bue - nos,*

G   **D7**

1. I say "Yes," my Lord, to
2. *Di - go "Si," Se - ñor, a*

D7   **G**

1. ev - 'ry word you speak.
2. *to - do lo que ha- blas.*

What Does It Mean to Follow Jesus?

CAPO 1st Fret

Refrain

What does it mean to fol-low Je-sus? What does it mean to

go his way? What does it mean to do what he wants me to,

to Verse

ev - 'ry day?

Last time

ev - 'ry day?

Peace Walk

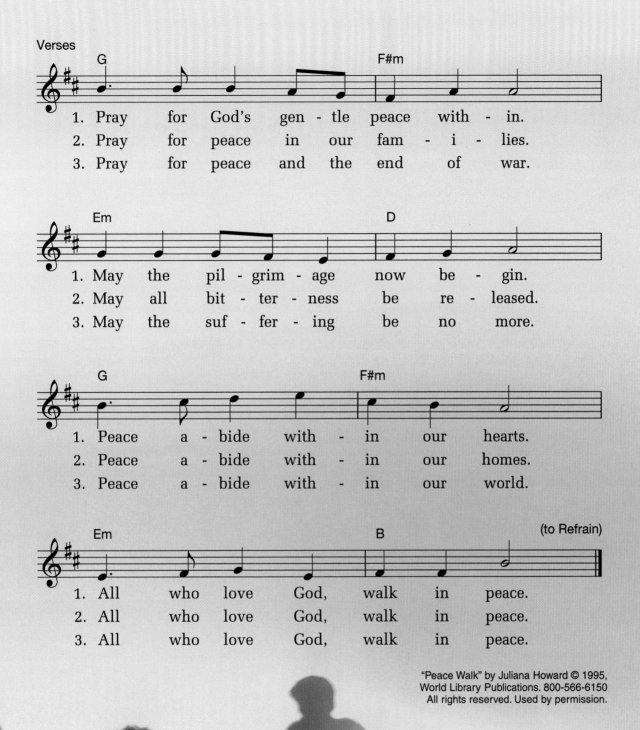

All You Works of God

Refrain

All you works of God, ev-'ry moun-tain, star and tree, bless the One

__ who shapes your beau-ty, who has caused you all to

be one great song of love and grace, ev-er an-cient, ev-er

new. Raise your voi-ces, all you works of God!

I am aware of God's love when I laugh!

Verses

1. Sun and moon: Bless your Mak - er! Stars of heav - en:
2. Winds of God: Bless your Mak - er! Cold and win - ter:
3. Wells and springs: Bless your Mak - er! Seas and riv - ers:
4. Fly - ing birds: Bless your Mak - er! Beasts and cat - tle:

1. Chant your praise! Show - ers and dew:
2. Chant your praise! Snow - storms and ice:
3. Chant your praise! Whales in the deep:
4. Chant your praise! Chil - dren at play:

(to Refrain)

1. Raise up your joy - ful song.
2. Raise up your joy - ful song.
3. Raise up your joy - ful song.
4. Raise up your joy - ful song.

I am aware of God's love when I sing!

I am aware of God's love when I dance!

Come, O Holy Spirit / Wa Wa Wa Emimimo

F   F

1. Come, O Ho – ly Spir – it, come.
2. Come, O Ho – ly Spir – it, come.
3. *Wa wa wa E – mi – mi – mo.*
4. *Wa wa wa E – mi – mi – mo.*

F   C

1. Come, Al – might – y Spir – it, come.
2. Come, Al – might – y Spir – it, come.
3. *Wa wa wa A – lag – ba – ra.*
4. *Wa wa wa A – lag – ba – ra.*

F   C   F

1. Come, come, come.
2. Come, come, come.
3. *Wa – o, wa – o, wa – o.*
4. *Wa – o, wa – o, wa – o.*

"Come, O Holy Spirit/Wa Wa Wa Emimimo" from traditional Nigerian text. English transcription and paraphrase © 1999 I-to-Loh (World Council of Churches).

Glossary

A

Abba an informal word for *Father* in the language Jesus spoke. Jesus called God the Father "Abba." [Abba]

absolution the forgiveness God offers us in the Sacrament of Penance. After we say that we are sorry for our sins, we receive God's absolution from the priest. [absolución]

absolution

Advent the four weeks before Christmas. It is a time of joyful preparation for the celebration of Jesus' birth as our Savior. [Adviento]

All Saints Day November 1, the day on which the Church honors all who have died and now live with God as saints in heaven. This group includes those who have been declared saints by the Church and many others known only to God. [Día de Todos los Santos]

All Souls Day November 2, the day on which the Church remembers all who have died as friends of God. We pray that they may rest in peace. [Día de Difuntos]

altar the table in the church on which the priest celebrates Mass, during which the sacrifice of Christ on the cross is made present in the Sacrament of the Eucharist. The altar represents two aspects of the mystery of the Eucharist. First, it is where Jesus Christ offers himself for our sins. Second, it is where he gives us himself as our food for eternal life. [altar]

ambo a raised stand from which a person reads the Word of God during Mass [ambón]

Amen the final word in any prayer. *Amen* means "This is true." When we pray "Amen," it shows that we really mean what we have just said. [Amén]

angel a spiritual creature who brings a message from God [ángel]

Annunciation the announcement to Mary by the angel Gabriel that God had chosen her to be the mother of Jesus [Anunciación]

Annunciation

Anointing of the Sick one of the seven sacraments. In this sacrament a sick person has holy oil applied and receives the strength, peace, and courage to overcome the difficulties that come with illness.
[unción de los enfermos]

apostle one of twelve special men who accompanied Jesus in his ministry and were witnesses to the Resurrection [apóstol]

Apostles' Creed a statement of Christian belief. The Apostles' Creed, developed out of a creed used in Baptism in Rome, lists simple statements of belief in God the Father, Jesus Christ the Son, and the Holy Spirit. The profession of faith used in Baptism today is based on the Apostles' Creed. [Credo de los Apóstoles]

apostolic one of the four Marks of the Church. The Church is apostolic because it hands on the teachings of the apostles through their successors, the bishops. [apostólica]

Ascension the return of Jesus to heaven. In the Acts of the Apostles, it is written that Jesus, after his Resurrection, spent 40 days on earth instructing his followers. He then returned to his Father in heaven. [Ascensión]

Ash Wednesday the first day of Lent, on which we receive ashes on our foreheads. The ashes remind us to prepare for Easter by showing sorrow for the choices we make that offend God and hurt our relationships with others. [Miércoles de Ceniza]

B

Baptism the first of the three sacraments by which we become members of the Church. Baptism frees us from original sin and gives us new life in Jesus Christ through the Holy Spirit. [bautismo]

baptismal font

Beatitudes the eight ways we can behave to live a blessed life. Jesus teaches us that if we live according to the Beatitudes, we will live a happy Christian life. [Bienaventuranzas]

Bible the history of God's promise to care for us and his call for us to be faithful to him. God asked that people be faithful first through the beliefs of the Jewish people and then through belief in the life, death, and resurrection of Jesus Christ. [Biblia]

bishop a man who has received the fullness of Holy Orders. He has inherited his duties from the original apostles. He cares for the Church today and is a principal teacher in the Church. [obispo]

Blessed Sacrament the bread that has been consecrated by the priest at Mass. It is kept in the tabernacle to adore and to be taken to the sick. [Santísimo Sacramento]

blessing a prayer that calls for God's power and care upon some person, place, thing, or special activity [bendición]

Body and Blood of Christ the bread and wine that has been consecrated by the priest at Mass. It still looks like bread and wine, but it is actually the Body and Blood of Jesus Christ. [Cuerpo y Sangre de Cristo]

C

capital sins those sins that can lead us to more serious sin. The seven capital sins are pride, covetousness, envy, anger, gluttony, lust, and sloth. [pecados capitales]

catholic one of the four Marks of the Church. The Church is catholic because Jesus is fully present in it and because Jesus has given the Church to the whole world. [católico]

charity a virtue given to us by God. Charity helps us love God above all things and our neighbor as ourselves. [caridad]

charity

Christ a title that means "anointed with oil." It is from a Greek word that means the same thing as the Hebrew word *Messiah*, or "anointed." It is the name given to Jesus after the Resurrection. [Cristo]

Christian the name given to all those who have been anointed through the gift of the Holy Spirit in Baptism and have become followers of Jesus Christ [cristiano]

Christmas the day on which we celebrate the birth of Jesus (December 25) [Navidad]

Church the name given to all of the followers of Christ throughout the world. It is also the name of the building where we gather to pray to God and the name of our community as we gather to praise God. [Iglesia]

commandment a standard, or rule, for living as God wants us to live. Jesus summarized all of the commandments into two: love God and love your neighbor. [mandamiento]

Communion of Saints the union of all who have been saved in Jesus Christ, both those who are alive and those who have died [Comunión de los Santos]

confession the act of telling our sins to a priest in the Sacrament of Penance. The sacrament itself is sometimes referred to as confession. [confesión]

confession

Confirmation the sacrament that completes the grace we receive in Baptism. Confirmation seals, or confirms, this grace through the seven gifts of the Holy Spirit that we receive as part of Confirmation. This sacrament also unites us more closely in Jesus Christ. [confirmación]

conscience the inner voice that helps each of us to know the law that God has placed in our hearts. It guides us to do good and avoid evil. [conciencia]

consecration the making of a thing or a person to be special to God through a prayer or blessing. At Mass the words of the priest are a consecration that makes Jesus Christ's Body and Blood present in the bread and wine. People or objects set apart for God in a special way are also consecrated. For example, churches and altars are consecrated for use in liturgy. In the same way, bishops are consecrated as they receive the fullness of the sacrament of Holy Orders. [consagración]

contrition the sorrow we feel when we know that we have sinned, followed by the decision not to sin again. Contrition is the most important part of our celebration of the Sacrament of Penance. [contrición]

conversion the change of heart that directs each person away from sin and toward God [conversión]

Corporal Works of Mercy kind acts by which we help our neighbors with their everyday, material needs. Corporal Works of Mercy include feeding the hungry, finding a home for the homeless, clothing the naked, visiting the sick and those in prison, giving alms to the poor, and burying the dead. [obras corporales de misericordia]

covenant a solemn agreement between people or between people and God. God made covenants with humanity through agreements with Noah, Abraham, and Moses. These covenants offered salvation. God's new and final covenant was established through Jesus' life, death, and resurrection. [alianza]

creation God's act of making everything that exists outside himself. Creation is everything that exists. God said that all of creation is good. [creación]

covenant

Creator God, who made everything that is and whom we can come to know through everything he created [Creador]

creed a brief summary of what people believe. The Apostles' Creed is a summary of Christian beliefs. [credo]

crozier the staff carried by a bishop. This staff shows that the bishop cares for us in the same way that a shepherd cares for his sheep. It also reminds us that he represents Jesus, the Good Shepherd. [báculo]

D

deacon a man ordained through the Sacrament of Holy Orders to help the bishop and priests in the work of the Church [diácono]

diocese the members of the Church in a particular area, gathered under the leadership of a bishop [diócesis]

Eucharist

disciple a person who has accepted Jesus' message and tries to live as he did [discípulo]

E

Easter the celebration of the bodily raising of Jesus Christ from the dead. Easter is the most important Christian feast. [Pascua]

Emmanuel a name from the Old Testament that means "God with us." Because Jesus is always with us, we often call him by the name *Emmanuel*. [Emanuel]

envy a feeling of resentment or sadness because someone has a quality, a talent, or a possession that we want. Envy is one of the seven capital sins, and it is contrary to the tenth commandment. [envidia]

Epiphany the day on which we celebrate the visit of the Magi to Jesus after his birth. This is the day that Jesus was revealed as the savior of the whole world. [Epifanía]

epistle a letter written by Saint Paul or another leader to a group of Christians in the early Church. Twenty-one of the 27 books of the New Testament are epistles. [epístola]

Eucharist the sacrament in which we give thanks to God for giving us Jesus Christ in the bread and wine that becomes the Body and Blood of Jesus. This sacrament brings us into union with Jesus and his saving death and resurrection. [Eucaristía]

examination of conscience the act of prayerfully thinking about what we have said or done that may have hurt our relationship with God or others. An examination of conscience is an important part of preparing to celebrate the Sacrament of Penance. [examen de conciencia]

F

faith a gift of God that helps us to believe in him and live as he wants us to live. We express our faith in the words of the Apostles' Creed. [fe]

fasting limiting the amount we eat for a period of time, to express sorrow for sin and to make ourselves more aware of God's action in our lives [ayuno]

forgiveness the willingness to be kind to people who have hurt us but have then said that they are sorry. Because God always forgives us when we say that we are sorry, we forgive others in the same way. [perdón]

fortitude the strength to do the right thing even when that is difficult. Fortitude is one of the four central human virtues, called the Cardinal Virtues, by which we guide our Christian life. It is also one of the Gifts of the Holy Spirit. [fortaleza]

free will our ability to choose to do good because God has made us like him [libre albedrío]

Fruits of the Holy Spirit the ways in which we act because God is alive in us [frutos del Espíritu Santo]

G

genuflect to show respect in church by touching a knee to the ground, especially when we are before the Blessed Sacrament in the tabernacle. [genuflexión, hacer la]

God the Father, Son, and Holy Spirit: one God in three distinct persons. God created us, saves us, and lives in us. [Dios]

godparent a witness to Baptism who helps the baptized person follow the path of Christian life [padrino/madrina de bautismo]

gospel the good news of God's mercy and love. We experience this news in the story of Jesus' life, death, and resurrection. The story is presented to us in four books in the New Testament: the Gospels of Matthew, Mark, Luke, and John. [Evangelio]

grace the gift of God given to us without our deserving it. Sanctifying grace fills us with his life and enables us always to be his friends. Grace also helps us to live as God wants us to. [gracia]

Great Commandment Jesus' essential teaching that we are to love both God and our neighbor as we love ourselves [El Mandamiento Mayor]

heaven, *Paradise*

H

heaven the life with God that is full of happiness and never ends [cielo]

holy one of the four Marks of the Church. It is the kind of life we live when we share in the life of God, who is all holiness. The Church is holy because of her union with Jesus Christ. [santa]

Holy Communion the consecrated bread and wine that we receive at Mass, which is the Body and Blood of Jesus Christ. It brings us into union with Jesus Christ and his saving death and resurrection. [Sagrada Comunión]

Holy Days of Obligation the principal feast days, other than Sundays, of the Church. On Holy Days of Obligation, we celebrate the great things that God has done for us through Jesus Christ and the saints. [días de precepto]

Holy Family the family made up of Jesus; his mother, Mary; and his foster father, Joseph [Sagrada Familia]

Holy Orders the sacrament through which the mission, or task, given by Jesus to his apostles continues in the Church. Holy Orders has three degrees: deacon, priest, and bishop. [orden sagrado]

Holy Spirit the third person of the Trinity, who is sent to us as our helper and, through Baptism and Confirmation, fills us with God's life [Espíritu Santo]

holy water the water that has been blessed and is used as a sacramental to remind us of our Baptism [agua bendita]

holy water

Holy Week the celebration of the events surrounding Jesus' suffering, death, resurrection, and establishment of the Eucharist. Holy Week commemorates Jesus' triumphal entry into Jerusalem on Palm Sunday, the gift of himself in the Eucharist on Holy Thursday, his death on Good Friday, and his resurrection at the Easter Vigil on Holy Saturday. [Semana Santa]

homily an explanation of God's Word. A homily explains the words of God that we hear in the Bible readings at church. [homilía]

hope the trust that God will always be with us. We also trust that he will make us happy now and help us to live in a way that keeps us with him forever. [esperanza]

J

Jesus the Son of God, who was born of the Virgin Mary and who died and was raised from the dead so that we can live with God forever. His name means "God saves." [Jesús]

Joseph the foster father of Jesus, who was engaged to Mary when the angel announced that Mary would have a child through the power of the Holy Spirit [José]

justice the strong, firm desire to give to God and others what is due them. Justice is one of the four central human virtues, called the Cardinal Virtues, by which we guide our Christian life. [justicia]

K

Kingdom of God God's rule over us. We experience the Kingdom of God in part now, and we will experience it fully in heaven. The Kingdom of God was announced in the Gospel and is present in the Eucharist. [Reino de Dios]

L

Last Supper the last meal Jesus ate with his disciples on the night before he died. At the Last Supper, Jesus took bread and wine, blessed it, and said that it was his Body and Blood. Every Mass is a remembrance of this last meal. [Última Cena]

Last Supper

Lectionary the book that contains all of the Bible stories we read at Mass [Leccionario]

Lent six weeks during which we prepare to celebrate, with special prayers and action, the rising of Jesus from the dead at Easter. Jesus rose from the dead to save us. [Cuaresma]

liturgy the public prayer of the Church that celebrates the wonderful things God has done for us in Jesus Christ [liturgia]

Liturgy of the Eucharist the second half of the Mass, in which the bread and wine are blessed and become the Body and Blood of Jesus Christ. We then receive the Body and Blood of Jesus Christ in Holy Communion. [Liturgia de la Eucaristía]

Liturgy of the Word the first half of the Mass, in which we listen to God's Word from the Bible and consider what it means for us today [Liturgia de la Palabra]

M

Magnificat Mary's song of praise to God for the great things he has done for her and planned for us through Jesus [Magníficat]

Marks of the Church the four most important things about the Church. The Church is one, holy, catholic, and apostolic. [calificados de la Iglesia]

Mary the mother of Jesus. She is called blessed and "full of grace" because God chose her to be the mother of the Son of God. [María]

Mass the most important sacramental celebration of the Church. The celebration of the Mass was established by Jesus at the Last Supper as a remembrance of his death and resurrection. At Mass we listen to God's Word from the Bible and receive Jesus Christ in the bread and wine that has been blessed to become his Body and Blood. [Misa]

matrimony a solemn agreement between a woman and a man to be partners for life, both for their own good and for rearing children. Marriage is a sacrament when the agreement is properly made between baptized Christians. [matrimonio]

Matrimony

Messiah a title that means "anointed with oil." It is from a Hebrew word that means the same thing as the Greek word *Christ*, the name given to Jesus after the Resurrection. [Mesías]

ministry service or work done for others. Ministry is also done by bishops, priests, and deacons in the celebration of the sacraments. All those baptized are called to different kinds of ministry in the liturgy and in service to the needs of others. [ministerio]

mission the work of Jesus Christ that is continued in the Church through the Holy Spirit. The mission of the Church is to proclaim salvation through Jesus' life, death, and resurrection. [misión]

monastery a place where men or women live out their solemn promises of poverty, chastity, and obedience. They live a stable, or firm, community life; and they spend their days in public prayer, work, and meditation. [monasterio]

Montserrat monastery

moral choice a choice to do what is right. We make moral choices because they are what we believe God wants. We make them also because we have the freedom to choose what is right and avoid what is wrong. [opción moral]

moral law a rule for living that has been established by God and people in authority who are concerned about the good of all people. Moral laws are based on God's direction to us to do what is right and avoid what is wrong. [ley moral]

mortal sin a serious decision to turn away from God by doing something that we know is wrong and so cuts us off from God's life [pecado mortal]

Mystical Body of Christ the members of the Church formed into a spiritual body and bound together by the life communicated by Jesus Christ through the sacraments. Christ is the center and source of the life of this body. In it, we are all are united. Each member of this body receives from Christ gifts fitting for him or her. [Cuerpo Místico de Cristo]

N

New Testament the 27 books of the second part of the Bible which tell of the teaching, ministry, and saving events of the life of Jesus. The four Gospels present Jesus' life, death, and resurrection. The Acts of the Apostles tells the story of the message of salvation as it spread through the growth of the Church. Various letters instruct us in how to live as followers of Jesus Christ. The Book of Revelation offers encouragement to Christians living through persecution. [Nuevo Testamento]

O

obedience the act of willingly following what God asks us to do for our salvation. The fourth commandment requires children to obey their parents, and all people are required to obey civil authority when it acts for the good of all. [obediencia]

oil of the sick the oil blessed by the bishop during Holy Week and used in the Sacrament of Anointing of the Sick, which brings spiritual and, if it is God's will, physical healing as well [óleo de los enfermos]

Old Testament the first 46 books of the Bible which tell of God's covenant with the people of Israel and his plan for the salvation of all people. The first five books are known as the Torah. The Old Testament is fulfilled in the New Testament, but God's covenant presented in the Old Testament has permanent value and has never been revoked, or set aside. [Antiguo Testamento]

one one of the four Marks of the Church. The Church is one because of its source in the one God and because of its founder, Jesus Christ. Jesus, through his death on the cross, united all to God in one body. Within the unity of the Church, there is great diversity because of the variety of the gifts given to its members. [una]

original sin the result of the sin by which the first human beings disobeyed God and chose to follow their own will rather than God's will. Because of this act, all human beings lost the original blessing that God had intended and they became subject to sin and death. In Baptism we are restored to life with God

Palm Sunday

through Jesus Christ. [pecado original]

P

Palm Sunday the celebration of Jesus' triumphant entry into Jerusalem on the Sunday before Easter. It begins a week-long commemoration of the saving events of Holy Week. [Domingo de Ramos]

parable one of the simple stories that Jesus told to show us what the Kingdom of God is like. Parables present images, or scenes, drawn from everyday life. These images show us the radical, or serious, choice we make when we respond to the invitation to enter the Kingdom of God. [parábola]

parish a community of believers in Jesus Christ who meet regularly in a specific area to worship God under the leadership of a pastor [parroquia]

Paschal Mystery the work of salvation accomplished by Jesus Christ through his passion, death, and resurrection. The Paschal Mystery is celebrated in the liturgy of the Church. Its saving effects are experienced by us in the sacraments. [Misterio Pascual]

pastor a priest who is responsible for the spiritual care of the members of a parish community [pastor]

penance the turning away from sin with a desire to change our life and more closely live the way God wants us to live. We express our penance externally by praying, fasting, and helping the poor. This is also the name of the action that the priest asks us take or the prayers that he asks us to pray after he absolves us in the Sacrament of Penance. (*See* Sacrament of Penance.) [penitencia]

pope

Pentecost the 50th day after Jesus was raised from the dead. On this day the Holy Spirit was sent from heaven, and the Church was born. [Pentecostés]

people of God another name for the Church. In the same way that the people of Israel were God's people through the Covenant he made with them, the Church is a priestly, prophetic, and royal people through the new and eternal Covenant in Jesus Christ. [Pueblo de Dios]

personal sin a sin we choose to commit, whether serious (mortal) or less serious (venial). Although the result of original sin is to leave us with a tendency to sin, God's grace, especially through the sacraments, helps us to choose good over sin. [pecado personal]

petition a request of God asking him to fulfill a need. When we share in God's saving love, we understand that every need is one that we can ask God to help us with through petition. [petición]

pope the bishop of Rome, successor of Saint Peter, and leader of the Roman Catholic Church. Because he has the authority to act in the name of Christ, the pope is called the Vicar of Christ. The pope and all of the bishops together make up the living, teaching office of the Church, the Magisterium. [Papa]

praise the expression of our response to God, not only for what he does, but simply because he is. In the Eucharist the whole Church joins with Jesus Christ in expressing praise and thanksgiving to the Father. [alabanza]

prayer the raising of our hearts and minds to God. We are able to speak to and listen to God in prayer because he teaches us how to do so. [oración]

Precepts of the Church those positive requirements that the pastoral authority of the Church has determined as necessary. These requirements describe the minimum effort we must make in prayer and the moral life. The Precepts of the Church ensure that all Catholics move beyond the minimum by growing in love of God and love of neighbor. [preceptos de la Iglesia]

pride a false image of ourselves that goes beyond what we deserve as God's creation. Pride puts us in competition with God. It is one of the seven capital sins. [soberbia]

priest a man who has accepted God's special call to serve the Church by guiding it and building it up through the celebration of the sacraments [sacerdote]

prudence the virtue that directs us toward the good. It also helps us to choose the correct means to achieve that good. Prudence is one of the Cardinal Virtues that guide our conscience and influence us to live according to the law of Christ. [prudencia]

psalm a prayer in the form of a poem. A psalm was written to be sung in public worship. Each psalm expresses an aspect, or feature, of the depth of human prayer. Over several centuries 150 psalms were gathered to form the Book of Psalms, used in worship in the Old Testament. [salmo]

R

reconciliation the renewal of friendship after that friendship has been broken by some action or lack of action. In the Sacrament of Penance, through God's mercy and forgiveness, we are reconciled with God, the Church, and others. [reconciliación]

Redeemer Jesus Christ, whose life, death on the cross, and resurrection from the dead set us free from sin and bring us redemption [Redentor]

redemption our being set free from sin through the life, death on the cross, and resurrection from the dead of Jesus Christ [redención]

repentance our turning away from sin with a desire to change our lives and live more closely as God wants us to live. We express our penance externally by prayer, fasting, and helping the poor. [arrepentimiento]

Resurrection the bodily raising of Jesus Christ from the dead on the third day after his death on the cross. The Resurrection is the crowning truth of our faith. [Resurrección]

Revelation God's communication of himself to us through the words and deeds he has used throughout history. Revelation shows us the mystery of his plan for our salvation in his Son, Jesus Christ. [revelación]

The Resurrection

rite one of the many forms followed in celebrating liturgy in the Church. A rite may differ according to the culture or country where it is celebrated. *Rite* also means the special form for celebrating each sacrament. [rito]

Rosary a prayer in honor of the Blessed Virgin Mary. When we pray the Rosary, we meditate on the mysteries of Jesus Christ's life while praying the Hail Mary on five sets of ten beads and the Lord's Prayer on the beads in between. [Rosario]

Rosary

S

sacrament one of seven ways through which God's life enters our lives through the work of the Holy Spirit. Jesus gave us three sacraments that bring us into the Church: Baptism, Confirmation, and the Eucharist. He gave us two sacraments that bring us healing: Penance and Anointing of the Sick. He also gave us two sacraments that help members serve the community: Matrimony and Holy Orders. [sacramento]

Sacrament of Penance the sacrament in which we celebrate God's forgiveness of our sins and our reconciliation with God and the Church. Penance includes sorrow for the sins we have committed,

confession of sins, absolution by the priest, and doing the penance that shows our sorrow. [sacramento de la penitencia]

sacramental an object, a prayer, or a blessing given by the Church to help us grow in our spiritual life [sacramental]

Sacraments of Initiation the sacraments that are the foundation of our Christian life. We are born anew in Baptism, strengthened by Confirmation, and receive in the Eucharist the food of eternal life. [sacramentos de iniciación]

Baptism

Confirmation

Eucharist

Sacrifice of the Mass the sacrifice of Jesus on the cross which is remembered and made present in the Eucharist [Sacrificio de la Misa]

saint a holy person who has died united with God. The Church has said that this person is now with God forever in heaven. [santo]

salvation the gift of forgiveness of sin and the restoration of friendship with God. God alone can give us salvation. [salvación]

Savior Jesus, the Son of God, who became human to forgive our sins and restore our friendship with God. *Jesus* means "God saves." [Salvador]

Scriptures the holy writings of Jews and Christians collected in the Old and New Testaments of the Bible [Sagrada Escritura]

Sermon on the Mount the words of Jesus, written in Chapters 5 through 7 of the Gospel of Matthew, in which Jesus reveals how he has fulfilled God's law given to Moses. The Sermon on the Mount begins with the eight Beatitudes and includes the Lord's Prayer. [Sermón de la Montaña]

sin a choice we make that offends God and hurts our relationships with other people. Some sin is mortal and needs to be confessed in the Sacrament of Penance. Other sin is venial, or less serious. [pecado]

sloth a carelessness of heart that leads a person to ignore his or her development as a person, especially spiritual development and a relationship with God. Sloth is one of the seven capital sins, and it is contrary to the first commandment. [pereza]

Son of God the title revealed by Jesus that indicates his unique relationship to God the Father [Hijo de Dios]

soul the part of us that makes us human and an image of God. Body and soul together form one unique human nature. The soul is responsible for our consciousness and for our freedom. [alma]

Spiritual Works of Mercy the kind acts through which we help our neighbors meet the needs that are more than material. The Spiritual Works of Mercy include instructing, advising, consoling, comforting, forgiving, and bearing wrongs with patience. [obras esprituales de misericordia]

Spiritual Works of Mercy

T

tabernacle a container in which the Blessed Sacrament is kept so that Holy Communion can be taken to the sick and the dying [sagrario]

temperance the Cardinal Virtue that helps us to control our attraction to pleasure so that our natural desires are kept within proper limits. This moral virtue helps us choose to use created goods in moderation. [templanza]

temptation an attraction, from outside us or from inside us, that can lead us to not follow God's commands [tentación]

Ten Commandments the ten rules that God gave to Moses on Mount Sinai that sum up God's law and show us what is required to love God and our neighbor
[Diez Mandamientos]

Theological Virtues those virtues given to us by God and not by human effort. They are faith, hope, and charity. [virtudes teologales]

Torah the Hebrew word for "instruction" or "law." It is also the name of the first five books of the Old Testament: Genesis, Exodus, Leviticus, Numbers, and Deuteronomy. [Torá]

trespasses an unlawful act committed against the property or rights of another person, or an act that physically harms a person [ofensas]

Trinity the mystery of one God existing in three persons: the Father, the Son, and the Holy Spirit [Trinidad]

Trinity

U

universal Church the entire Church as it exists throughout the world. The people of every diocese, along with their bishops and the pope, make up the universal Church.
[Iglesia universal]

V

venial sin a choice we make that weakens our relationship with God or other people. It wounds and diminishes the divine life in us.
[pecado venial]

viaticum the Eucharist that a dying person receives. It is spiritual food for the last journey we make as Christians, the journey through death to eternal life. [viático]

Vicar of Christ the title given to the pope who, as the successor of Saint Peter, has the authority to act in Christ's place. A vicar is someone who stands in for and acts for another.
[Vicario de Cristo]

virtue an attitude or way of acting that helps us do good [virtud]

Visitation Mary's visit to Elizabeth to share the good news that Mary is to be the mother of Jesus. Elizabeth's greeting of Mary forms part of the Hail Mary. During this visit, Mary sings the Magnificat, her praise of God.
[Visitación]

vocation the call each of us has in life to be the person God wants each to be and the way we serve the Church and the Kingdom of God. Each of us can live out his or her vocation as a layperson, as a member of a religious community, or as a member of the clergy. [vocación]

W

witness the passing on to others, by our words and by our actions, the faith that we have been given. Every Christian has the duty to give witness to the good news about Jesus Christ that he or she has come to know. [testimonio]

worship the adoration and honor given to God in public prayer [culto]

worship

Glosario

A

Abba palabra que significa "padre" en el idioma que hablaba Jesús. Jesús llamaba a Dios Padre *Abba*. [Abba]

absolución perdón que Dios nos ofrece en el sacramento de la penitencia. Después de que decimos que nos arrepentimos de nuestros pecados, recibimos del sacerdote la absolución de Dios. [absolution]

Adviento las cuatro semanas antes de la Navidad. Es una época de jubilosa preparación para la celebración del nacimiento de Jesús, como salvador nuestro. [Advent]

agua bendita agua que ha sido bendecida y que se usa como sacramental para recordarnos de nuestro bautismo [holy water]

alabanza la expresión de nuestra respuesta a Dios, no sólo por lo que hace sino por quién es. En la Eucaristía, la Iglesia entera se une a Jesucristo para alabar y dar gracias al Padre. [praise]

alianza pacto solemne que hacen las personas entre sí o que hacen las personas con Dios. Dios hizo alianzas con la humanidad mediante los pactos hechos con Noé, Abraham, y Moisés. Estas alianzas ofrecían salvación. La nueva y final alianza de Dios fue pactada mediante la vida, muerte y resurrección de Jesús. [covenant]

alma parte de la persona que la hace humana e imagen de Dios. Juntos, el cuerpo y el alma forman una naturaleza humana única. El alma es responsable de nuestra conciencia y de nuestra libertad. [soul]

altar mesa que tienen las iglesias en la que el sacerdote celebra la Misa. En la Misa, el sacrificio de Cristo en la cruz se hace presente en el sacramento de la Eucaristía. El altar representa dos aspectos del misterio de la Eucaristía: en primer lugar, es el sitio donde Jesucristo se ofrece a sí mismo por nuestros pecados; y, en segundo, es el sitio donde Él se da a nosotros como alimento de vida eterna. [altar]

ambón plataforma elevada desde donde una persona lee la Palabra de Dios durante la Misa [ambo]

Amén palabra final de toda oración que significa "es verdad". Al decir *Amén*, damos a entender que lo que acabamos de decir va en serio. [Amen]

ángel criatura espiritual que trae mensajes de Dios [angel]

Antiguo Testamento los 46 primeros libros de la Biblia que hablan de la alianza de Dios con el pueblo de Israel y su plan de salvación para toda la gente. Los cinco primeros libros se conocen como el Torá. El Antiguo Testamento se cumple en el Nuevo Testamento, pero la alianza de Dios presentada en el Antiguo Testamento sigue teniendo un valor permanente y nunca ha sido revocada, o anulada. [Old Testament]

Anunciación anuncio traído a María por el ángel Gabriel de que Dios la había elegido para ser madre de Jesús [Annunciation]

apóstol uno de doce hombres singulares que acompañaron a Jesús en su ministerio y fueron testigos de su Resurrección [apostle]

apostólica uno de los cuatro calificados de la Iglesia. La Iglesia es apostólica porque transmite las enseñanzas de los apóstoles a través de sus sucesores, los obispos. [apostolic]

arrepentimiento el apartarnos del pecado con el deseo de cambiar nuestra vida y acercarnos más a la forma de vida que Dios quiere que vivamos. Expresamos externamente nuestra penitencia mediante la oración, el ayuno, y ayudando a los pobres. [repentance]

Ascensión regreso de Jesús al cielo. En los Hechos de los Apóstoles, se escribe que, después de la Resurrección, Jesús estuvo 40 días en la Tierra instruyendo a sus seguidores, y luego volvió al cielo junto a su Padre. [Ascension]

ayuno limitar la cantidad de alimento que comemos por un tiempo determinado para expresar arrepentimiento por nuestros pecados y hacernos más conscientes de la acción de Dios en nuestras vidas [fasting]

B

báculo cayado o vara que lleva el obispo. Al llevar este cayado, el obispo muestra que cuida de nosotros de la misma forma en que el pastor cuida sus ovejas. También nos recuerda que él representa a Jesús, el Buen Pastor. [crozier]

bautismo el primero de los tres sacramentos mediante los cuales pasamos a ser miembros de la Iglesia. El bautismo nos libera del pecado original y nos da una vida nueva en Jesucristo por medio del Espíritu Santo. [Baptism]

bendición oración que invoca el poder y amparo de Dios para una persona, lugar, cosa, o una actividad específica [blessing]

Biblia historia escrita de la promesa que hizo Dios de cuidar de nosotros y de su llamado a que le seamos fieles. Dios pidió a la gente que le fuera fiel: primero, a través de las creencias del pueblo judío; y, luego, a través de la creencia en la vida, muerte, y resurrección de Jesucristo. [Bible]

Bienaventuranzas ocho explicaciones que nos dicen lo que significa llevar una vida bienaventurada. Jesús nos enseña que, si vivimos según las Bienaventuranzas, tendremos una vida cristiana dichosa. [Beatitudes]

C

calificados de la Iglesia las cuatro características más importantes de la Iglesia. La Iglesia es una, santa, católica y apostólica. [Marks of the Church]

caridad virtud dada a nosotros por Dios. La caridad nos permite amar a Dios sobre todas las cosas y al prójimo como a nosotros mismos. [charity]

católica uno de los calificados de la Iglesia. La Iglesia es católica porque Jesús está totalmente presente en ella y porque Jesús la ha dado al mundo entero. [catholic]

cielo vida con Dios que está llena de felicidad y que nunca termina [heaven]

Comunión de los Santos unidad de todos los que se han salvado en Jesucristo, ya sean vivos o muertos [Communion of Saints]

conciencia voz interior que nos ayuda a cada uno a conocer la ley que Dios ha colocado en nuestros corazones. La conciencia nos guía a hacer el bien y evitar el mal. [conscience]

confesión acto de contar nuestros pecados al sacerdote en el sacramento de la penitencia. Al sacramento mismo se le suele llamar "confesión". [confession]

confirmación sacramento que da plenitud a la gracia que recibimos en el bautismo. La confirmación sella, o confirma, esta gracia a través de los siete dones del Espíritu Santo que recibimos como parte de la confirmación. Este sacramento también nos une de forma más íntima en Jesucristo. [Confirmation]

consagración el hacer a una cosa o persona especial ante los ojos de Dios por medio de una oración o bendición. En la Misa, las palabras del sacerdote son una consagración que hace que el Cuerpo y Sangre de Cristo se hagan presentes en el pan y el vino. Las personas y objetos dedicados a Dios de forma especial también son consagrados. Por ejemplo, las iglesias y altares son consagrados para su uso en la liturgia. Del mismo modo, los obispos son consagrados al recibir la integridad del sacramento del orden sagrado. [consecration]

contrición pesar que sentimos cuando sabemos que hemos pecado, seguido por la decisión de no volver a pecar. La contrición es la parte más importante de nuestra celebración del sacramento de la penitencia. [contrition]

conversión cambio de vida que nos aparta del pecado y nos dirige a Dios [conversion]

creación el acto en que Dios hace todo lo que existe fuera de Él. Es todo lo que existe. Dios dijo que todo lo creado es bueno. [creation]

Creador Dios, quien hizo todo lo que es y a quien podemos llegar a conocer a través de todo lo que Él creó [Creator]

credo breve resumen de lo que cree la gente. El Credo de los Apóstoles es un resumen de la creencia cristiana. [creed]

Credo de los Apóstoles declaración de la creencia cristiana, originada de un credo usado en los bautismos en la ciudad de Roma. El Credo de los Apóstoles enumera sencillas declaraciones de la creencia en Dios Padre, su Hijo Jesucristo, y el Espíritu Santo. La profesión de fe usada actualmente en el bautismo se basa en este credo. [Apostles' Creed]

Understanding the Words of Our Faith **299**

cristiano nombre dado a todos los que han sido ungidos por medio del don del Espíritu Santo en el bautismo y se han convertido en seguidores de Jesucristo [Christian]

Cristo título que quiere decir "ungido". Proviene de una palabra griega que quiere decir lo mismo que el vocablo hebreo *Mesías* o "ungido". *Cristo* es el nombre que se le da a Jesús después de su Resurrección. [Christ]

Cuaresma las seis semanas en las que nos preparamos a celebrar en la Pascua la resurrección de Jesús de entre los muertos con oraciones y acciones especiales. Jesús resucitó para salvarnos. [Lent]

Cuerpo Místico de Cristo miembros de la Iglesia que forman un cuerpo espiritual y están unidos por la vida comunicada por Jesucristo a través de los sacramentos. Cristo es el centro y la fuente de la vida de este cuerpo. En él, todos estamos unidos. Cada miembro de este cuerpo recibe de Cristo dones que mas conviene a esa persona. [Mystical Body of Christ]

Cuerpo y Sangre de Cristo pan y vino que han sido consagrados por el sacerdote en la Misa. Aunque su aspecto sigue siendo de pan y vino, son en realidad el Cuerpo y Sangre de Jesucristo. [Body and Blood of Christ]

culto adoración y honor que se le rinde a Dios en oración pública [worship]

D

Día de Difuntos el 2 de noviembre, día en que la Iglesia conmemora a todos los que han muerto estando en amistad con Dios. Nosotros rezamos por ellos para que descansen en paz. [All Souls Day]

Día de Todos los Santos el 1 de noviembre, día en que la Iglesia conmemora a todos los muertos que pasaron a ser santos y ahora viven con Dios en el cielo. Entre éstos figuran todos aquéllos que han sido declarados santos por la Iglesia y muchos otros que sólo Dios conoce. [All Saints Day]

diácono varón ordenado mediante el sacramento del orden sagrado a asistir al obispo y a los sacerdotes en el trabajo de la Iglesia [deacon]

días de precepto principales días de fiesta de la Iglesia, exceptuando los domingos. En los días de precepto celebramos las grandes cosas que Dios ha hecho por nosotros a través de Jesucristo y los Santos. [Holy Days of Obligation]

Diez Mandamientos diez reglas que Dios dio a Moisés en el Monte Sinaí que resumen la ley de Dios y nos muestran lo que hay que hacer para amar a Dios y al prójimo [Ten Commandments]

diócesis miembros de la Iglesia de una zona determinada, congregados bajo la guía de un obispo [diocese]

Dios Padre, Hijo, y Espíritu Santo: un solo Dios en tres personas distintas. Dios nos creó; Él nos salva y vive en nosotros. [God]

discípulo persona que ha aceptado el mensaje de Jesús y trata de vivir de la misma forma en que Él vivió [disciple]

Domingo de Ramos celebración de la entrada triunfal de Jesús en Jerusalén que se hace el domingo antes de la Pascua. Esta celebración inicia una semana de conmemoración de los eventos de salvación de la Semana Santa. [Palm Sunday]

E

Emanuel nombre del Antiguo Testamento que significa "Dios con nosotros". Como Jesús está siempre con nosotros, lo llamamos por el nombre de *Emanuel*. [Emmanuel]

envidia sentimiento de resentimiento o tristeza debido a que alguien tiene una cualidad, talento o pertenencia que queremos. La envidia es uno de los siete pecados capitales y va en contra del décimo mandamiento. [envy]

Epifanía día en que se celebra la visita de los Reyes Magos a Jesús recién nacido. Éste es el día en que se revela a Jesús como Salvador del mundo entero. [Epiphany]

epístola carta escrita por San Pablo u otro guía espiritual a un grupo de cristianos en los primeros tiempos de la Iglesia. Veintiuno de los veintisiete libros del Nuevo Testamento son Epístolas. [epistle]

esperanza confianza de que Dios estará siempre con nosotros, nos dará felicidad ahora, y nos ayudará a vivir de forma que vivamos con Él para siempre [hope]

Espíritu Santo tercera persona de la Trinidad, que es enviada a nosotros para asistirnos y, mediante el bautismo y la confirmación, nos llena de la vida de Dios [Holy Spirit]

Eucaristía sacramento en el cual damos gracias a Dios por habernos dado a Jesucristo en el pan y el vino que se convierten en el Cuerpo y Sangre de Jesús. Este sacramento nos hace entrar en unión con Jesús y su muerte y resurrección redentoras. [Eucharist]

Evangelio buena nueva de la misericordia y amor de Dios. Nosotros experimentamos esta buena nueva en la historia de la vida, muerte y resurrección de Jesús. Esta historia se nos presenta en el Nuevo Testamento en cuatro libros: los Evangelios de San Mateo, San Marcos, San Lucas, y San Juan. [gospel]

examen de conciencia acto de reflexionar en oración sobre aquello que hemos dicho o hecho que pudo haber dañado nuestra amistad con Dios y con otras personas. El examen de conciencia es una parte importante de la preparación para la celebración del sacramento de la penitencia. [examination of conscience]

F

fe don de Dios. La fe nos permite creer en Dios y vivir de la forma en que Él quiere que vivamos. Expresamos nuestra fe con las palabras del Credo de los Apóstoles. [faith]

fortaleza fuerza que nos ayuda a obrar bien aun cuando sea difícil hacerlo. La fortaleza es una de las cuatro virtudes humanas centrales, llamadas virtudes cardinales, por las cuales guiamos nuestra vida cristiana. Es también uno de los dones del Espíritu Santo. [fortitude]

frutos del Espíritu Santo formas en que actuamos porque Dios está vivo en nosotros [Fruits of the Holy Spirit]

G

genuflexión, hacer la forma de mostrar respeto en la iglesia doblando una rodilla y haciéndola tocar el suelo, sobre todo cuando estamos ante el Santísimo Sacramento que está en el sagrario [genuflect]

gracia don de Dios que se nos da gratuitamente. La gracia sanctificante nos llena de su vida y permite que seamos siempre amigos suyos. La gracia también nos ayuda a vivir de la forma en que Dios quiere que vivamos. [grace]

H

Hijo de Dios título revelado por Jesús que indica su relación única con Dios Padre [Son of God]

homilía explicación de la Palabra de Dios. La homilía explica las palabras de Dios que oímos durante las lecturas de la Biblia en la iglesia. [homily]

I

Iglesia pueblo de Dios congregado en el mundo entero como seguidores de Jesús. Es también el nombre del edificio donde nos reunimos para orar a Dios y el de nuestra comunidad reunida para alabar a Dios. [Church]

Iglesia universal toda la Iglesia tal como existe en el mundo entero. La gente de cada diócesis, junto con sus obispos y el Papa, forman la Iglesia universal. [universal Church]

J

Jesús hijo de Dios, que nació de la Virgen María y murió y fue resucitado de entre los muertos para que pudiésemos vivir con Dios para siempre. Su nombre significa "Dios salva". [Jesus]

José padre adoptivo de Jesús, que estaba desposado con María cuando el ángel anunció que ella tendría un hijo por obra del poder del Espíritu Santo [Joseph]

justicia deseo firme y poderoso de dar a Dios y a los demás lo que les corresponde. Es una de las cuatro virtudes humanas centrales, llamadas virtudes cardinales, por las cuales guiamos nuestra vida cristiana. [justice]

L

Leccionario libro que contiene los distintos relatos bíblicos que se leen en la Misa [Lectionary]

ley moral regla de vida establecida por Dios y por personas de autoridad que se preocupan por el bien de todos. Las opciones morales se basan en la directiva que nos dio Dios de hacer lo que está bien y evitar lo que está mal. [moral law]

libre albedrío capacidad de optar por hacer el bien porque Dios nos ha hecho semejantes a Él [free will]

liturgia oración pública de la Iglesia que celebra las maravillas que Dios ha hecho por nosotros en Jesucristo [liturgy]

Liturgia de la Eucaristía la segunda de las dos partes de la Misa. En esta parte, se bendice el pan y el vino, que se convierten en Cuerpo y Sangre de Jesucristo. Luego, recibimos el Cuerpo y Sangre de Cristo en la Sagrada Comunión. [Liturgy of the Eucharist]

Liturgia de la Palabra la primera de las dos partes de la Misa. Durante esta parte, oímos la Palabra de Dios en la Biblia y reflexionamos sobre lo que significa hoy para nosotros. [Liturgy of the Word]

M

Magníficat canto de María de alabanza a Dios. Ella lo alaba por las grandes cosas que ha hecho por ella y los grandes planes que ha hecho para nosotros a través de Jesús. [Magnificat]

mandamiento norma, o regla, para vivir de la forma en que Dios quiere que vivamos. Jesús resumió todos los mandamientos en dos: amar a Dios y amar al prójimo. [commandment]

El Mandamiento Mayor enseñanza esencial de Jesús de amar a Dios y al prójimo como a nosotros mismos [Great Commandment]

María madre de Jesús. Se le dice bendita y "llena de gracia" porque Dios la eligió para ser madre del Hijo de Dios. [Mary]

matrimonio contrato solemne entre un varón y una mujer para ser compañeros por toda la vida, tanto para su bien propio como para procrear hijos. El matrimonio es un sacramento cuando el contrato se hace de forma apropiada entre cristianos bautizados. [matrimony]

Mesías nombre que quiere decir "ungido". Proviene de un vocablo hebreo que significa lo mismo que la palabra griega *Cristo*, que es el nombre dado a Jesús después de su resurrección. [Messiah]

Miércoles de Ceniza primer día de Cuaresma, en el que se nos coloca ceniza en la frente para que nos acordemos de que, para prepararnos para la Pascua, debemos mostrar arrepentimiento por decisiones que hemos tomado que ofenden a Dios y dañan nuestra relación con los demás [Ash Wednesday]

ministerio servicio, u obra, que se hace a otros. Lo hacen los obispos, sacerdotes, y diáconos en la celebración de los sacramentos. Todos los bautizados son llamados a distintos tipos de ministerio en la liturgia y en el servicio a las necesidades de los demás. [ministry]

Misa la celebración sacramental más importante de la Iglesia. La celebración de la Misa fue instituida por Jesús en la Última Cena para que fuera un recordatorio de su muerte y resurrección. En la Misa, oímos la Palabra de Dios en la Biblia y recibimos a Jesucristo en el pan y el vino que han sido consagrados para convertirse en su Cuerpo y Sangre. [Mass]

misión obra de Jesucristo que continúa en la Iglesia a través del Espíritu Santo. Proclama la salvación en la vida, muerte, y resurrección de Jesús. [mission]

Misterio Pascual obra de salvación realizada por Jesucristo mediante su pasión, muerte, y resurrección. El Misterio Pascual se celebra en la liturgia de la Iglesia. En los sacramentos experimentamos sus efectos redentores. [Paschal Mystery]

monasterio lugar donde viven varones o mujeres cumpliendo sus promesas solemnes de pobreza, castidad, y obediencia. Éstos viven una vida de comunidad estable, o firme; y pasan sus días en oración pública, trabajo, y meditación. [monastery]

N

Navidad día en que se festeja el nacimiento de Jesús (el 25 de diciembre) [Christmas]

Nuevo Testamento los veintisiete libros de la segunda parte de la Biblia, que relatan las enseñanzas, ministerio, y acontecimientos de salvación de la vida de Jesús. El Nuevo Testamento se compone de: cuatro Evangelios, que presentan la vida, muerte, y resurrección de Jesús; los Hechos de los Apóstoles, que narran la historia del mensaje de salvación al irse extendiendo con el crecimiento de la Iglesia; varias cartas que nos instruyen sobre cómo vivir como seguidores de Jesús; y el Libro del Apocalipsis, que da ánimo a los cristianos que sufren persecución. [New Testament]

O

obediencia acto de seguir por voluntad propia lo que Dios nos pide que hagamos para nuestra salvación. Según el cuarto mandamiento, los niños deben obedecer a sus padres; y todas las personas deben obedecer a la autoridad civil cuando obra en beneficio de todos. [obedience]

obispo varón que ha recibido el orden sagrado en su totalidad. Sus deberes los ha heredado de los primeros apóstoles. El obispo vela por la Iglesia y es un educador importante dentro de la Iglesia. [bishop]

obras corporales de misericordia buenas acciones con las que ayudamos a nuestro prójimo a cubrir sus necesidades materiales cotidianas. Las obras corporales de misericordia son: dar de comer al hambriento, dar techo al que no lo tiene, vestir al desnudo, visitar a los enfermos y a los presos, dar limosna a los pobres, y enterrar a los muertos. [Corporal Works of Mercy]

obras espirituales de misericordia
acciones caritativas mediante las
cuales socorremos al prójimo en sus
necesidades que van más allá de lo
material. Las obras espirituales de
misericordia son: instruir, aconsejar,
consolar, confortar, perdonar, y sufrir
con paciencia las flaquezas ajenas.
[Spiritual Works of Mercy]

ofensas actos contrarios a la ley
cometidos contra la propiedad o los
derechos de otra persona, o actos que
físicamente lastiman a esa persona
[trespasses]

óleo de los enfermos óleo bendecido
por el obispo durante la Semana
Santa y usado en el sacramento de la
unción de los enfermos, la cual brinda
sanación espiritual y, si Dios quiere,
sanación física también
[oil of the sick]

opción moral el elegir hacer lo que
está bien. Elegimos opciones morales
porque son lo que creemos que Dios
quiere. También las elegimos porque
tenemos la libertad de escoger lo que
está bien y evitar lo que está mal.
[moral choice]

oración el levantar el corazón y
la mente a Dios. Podemos hablar y
escuchar a Dios porque Él nos enseña
a orar. [prayer]

orden sagrado sacramento mediante
el cual la misión, o deber, dado por
Jesús a sus apóstoles continúa en la
Iglesia. El orden sagrado tiene tres
grados: diácono, sacerdote, y obispo.
[Holy Orders]

P

padrino/madrina de bautismo testigo
de bautismo que ayuda al bautizado a
seguir el camino de la vida cristiana
[godparent]

Papa el obispo de Roma, sucesor
de San Pedro, y cabeza de la Iglesia
Católica Romana. Como tiene autoridad
de actuar en nombre de Cristo, al Papa
se le llama Vicario de Cristo. El Papa
junto a todos los obispos conforma el
oficio de enseñanza viviente de la
Iglesia: el Magisterio. [pope]

parábola una de las sencillas
narraciones que Jesús contaba que
nos muestran cómo es el Reino de
Dios. Las parábolas nos presentan
imágenes, o escenas, tomadas de la
vida cotidiana. Estas imágenes nos
muestran la decisión radical, o seria,
que tomamos cuando respondemos a
la invitación de entrar en el Reino de
Dios. [parable]

parroquia comunidad de creyentes en
Jesucristo que se reúne regularmente
en una zona determinada para rendirle
culto a Dios bajo la guía de un pastor
[parish]

Pascua celebración de la resurrección
corporal de Jesucristo de entre los
muertos. La Pascua es la fiesta
cristiana más importante. [Easter]

pastor sacerdote responsable del
cuidado espiritual de los miembros
de una comunidad parroquial [pastor]

pecado decisión que tomamos que daña nuestra amistad con Dios y con los demás. Algunos pecados son mortales y deben ser confesados en el sacramento de la penitencia. Otros son veniales, o menos graves. [sin]

pecado mortal decisión grave de apartarnos de Dios haciendo algo que sabemos que está mal y que nos separa de la vida de Dios [mortal sin]

pecado original resultado del pecado por el cual los primeros seres humanos desobedecieron a Dios y decidieron seguir su propia voluntad y no la de Dios. A raíz de este acto, todos los seres humanos perdieron la bendición original que Dios les había destinado. Se sometieron al pecado y la muerte. En el bautismo, se nos restaura la vida con Dios a través de Jesucristo. [original sin]

pecado personal pecado que decidimos cometer. Puede ser grave (mortal) o menos grave (venial). Aunque las consecuencias del pecado original nos dejan con una tendencia al pecado, la gracia de Dios, sobre todo a través de los sacramentos, nos ayuda a elegir el bien sobre el mal. [personal sin]

pecado venial decisión que tomamos que debilita nuestra relación con Dios y los demás. El pecado venial hiere y reduce la vida divina que hay en nosotros. [venial sin]

pecados capitales aquellos pecados que pueden llevarnos a cometer pecados más graves. Los siete pecados capitales son: soberbia, avaricia, envidia, ira, gula, lujuria, y pereza. [capital sins]

penitencia el apartarnos del pecado con el deseo de cambiar nuestras vidas y acercarnos más a la forma de vida que Dios quiere que vivamos. Expresamos externamente nuestra penitencia mediante la oración, el ayuno, y ayudando a los pobres. También se le llama penitencia a la acción que el sacerdote nos pide hacer o a las oraciones que nos pide rezar después de que él nos absuelve en el sacramento de la penitencia. (*Véase* sacramento de la penitencia.) [penance]

Pentecostés el 50º día después de la resurrección de Jesús. En este día, el Espíritu Santo fue enviado del cielo y nació la Iglesia. [Pentecost]

perdón voluntad de ser benignos con una persona que nos ha hecho daño pero que después dice que está arrepentida. Como Dios siempre nos perdona cuando decimos que estamos arrepentidos, nosotros perdonamos de igual modo a los demás. [forgiveness]

pereza dejadez de corazón que lleva a una persona a no hacer caso de su desarrollo como persona, en particular de su desarrollo espiritual y de su relación con Dios. La pereza es uno de los siete pecados capitales, y va en contra del primer mandamiento. [sloth]

petición el pedir a Dios lo que necesitamos porque Él nos ha creado y quiere darnos lo que necesitamos. Cuando participamos del amor redentor de Dios, entendemos que para cada una de nuestras necesidades podemos pedirle a Dios que nos ayude mediante una petición. [petition]

preceptos de la Iglesia aquellos requisitos positivos que la autoridad pastoral de la Iglesia ha determinado como necesarios. Estos requisitos representan el esfuerzo mínimo que debemos hacer en la oración y en la vida moral. Los preceptos de la Iglesia se aseguran de que todos los católicos progresemos más allá del mínimo, creciendo en amor a Dios y en amor al prójimo. [Precepts of the Church]

prudencia virtud que nos orienta al bien. También nos ayuda a escoger los medios apropiados para alcanzar ese bien. La prudencia es una de las virtudes cardinales que guía nuestra conciencia e influye en nosotros para que vivamos según la ley de Cristo. [prudence]

Pueblo de Dios otro de los nombres de la Iglesia. Al igual que el pueblo de Israel era el pueblo de Dios debido a la alianza que hizo con ellos, la Iglesia es un pueblo sacerdotal, profético, y regio gracias a la nueva y eterna alianza en Jesucristo. [People of God]

R

reconciliación reanudar la amistad que se había roto por alguna acción o falta de acción. En el sacramento de la penitencia, mediante la misericordia y perdón de Dios, nos reconciliamos con Él, la Iglesia y los demás. [reconciliation]

redención el liberarnos del pecado mediante la vida, muerte en la cruz y resurrección de Jesucristo de entre los muertos [redemption]

Redentor Jesucristo, cuya vida, muerte en la cruz, y resurrección de entre los muertos nos libró del pecado y nos trajo la redención [Redeemer]

Reino de Dios el dominio de Dios sobre nosotros. Experimentamos hoy el Reino de Dios en parte, pero lo experimentaremos en su totalidad en el cielo. El Reino de Dios fue anunciado en el Evangelio y está presente en la Eucaristía. [Kingdom of God]

Resurrección el volver a la vida el cuerpo de Jesucristo el tercer día después de haber muerto en la cruz. La Resurrección es la verdad culminante de nuestra fe. [Resurrection]

revelación comunicación que nos hace Dios de sí por medio de las palabras y hechos que ha usado a lo largo de la historia. La revelación nos muestra el misterio del plan de salvación que tiene para nosotros en su Hijo, Jesucristo. [Revelation]

rito una de diversas formas de celebrar la liturgia en la Iglesia. Los ritos pueden ser distintos según la cultura o el país donde se celebre. *Rito* también quiere decir el modo especial en que celebramos cada sacramento. [rite]

Rosario oración en honor a la Virgen María. En el rezo del rosario, meditamos los misterios de la vida de Jesucristo rezando el Avemaría en los cinco grupos de diez cuentas y el Padrenuestro en las cuentas que van en medio. [Rosary]

S

sacerdote varón que ha aceptado un llamado especial para servir a la Iglesia guiándola y edificándola mediante la celebración de los sacramentos [priest]

sacramental objeto, oración, o bendición dados por la Iglesia que nos ayudan a crecer en nuestra vida espiritual [sacramental]

sacramento una de las siete formas en que la vida de Dios entra en nuestras vidas a través de la obra del Espíritu Santo. Jesús dio a nosotros tres sacramentos que nos hacen entrar en la Iglesia (bautismo, confirmación, y Eucaristía); dos sacramentos que nos traen sanación (penitencia y unción de los enfermos); y dos sacramentos que ayudan a los miembros a servir a la comunidad (matrimonio y orden sagrado). [sacrament]

sacramento de la penitencia sacramento en el cual celebramos el perdón de Dios a nuestros pecados y nuestra reconciliación con Él y la Iglesia. La penitencia consiste en el arrepentimiento de los pecados cometidos, la confesión de los pecados, la absolución por el sacerdote, y el cumplimiento de la penitencia para mostrar nuestro arrepentimiento. [Sacrament of Penance]

sacramentos de iniciación sacramentos que son los cimientos de nuestra vida cristiana. Volvemos a nacer en el bautismo, nos fortalecemos en el sacramento de la confirmación, y recibimos en la Eucaristía el alimento de la vida eterna. [Sacraments of Initiation]

Sacrificio de la Misa sacrificio de Jesús en la cruz, el cual se recuerda y se hace presente en la Eucaristía [Sacrifice of the Mass]

Sagrada Comunión pan y vino consagrados que recibimos en la Misa, los cuales son bendecidos y se convierten en el Cuerpo y Sangre de Jesucristo. La Sagrada Comunión nos hace entrar en unión con Jesucristo y su muerte y resurrección redentoras. [Holy Communion]

Sagrada Escritura escritos sagrados de los judíos y cristianos recopilados en el Antiguo y Nuevo Testamento de la Biblia [Scriptures]

Sagrada Familia familia compuesta por Jesús, su madre María y su padre adoptivo José [Holy Family]

sagrario pieza donde se guarda el Santísimo Sacramento consagrado para que la Sagrada Comunión pueda ser llevada a los enfermos y moribundos [tabernacle]

salmo oración en forma de poema. Los salmos estaban destinados para ser cantados en cultos públicos. Cada salmo expresa un aspecto, o característica, de la profundidad de la oración humana. A lo largo de varios siglos, se han recolectado 150 salmos que forman el Libro de los Salmos. Estos salmos se usaban en el culto a Dios en el Antiguo Testamento. [psalm]

salvación don del perdón del pecado y la reanudación de la amistad con Dios. Sólo Dios puede darnos salvación. [salvation]

Salvador Jesús, el Hijo de Dios, que se hizo hombre para perdonar nuestros pecados y reanudar nuestra amistad con Dios. *Jesús* quiere decir "Dios salva". [Savior]

santa uno de los cuatro calificados de la Iglesia. Es el tipo de vida que vivimos cuando participamos de la vida de Dios, que es todo santidad. La Iglesia es santa por su unión con Jesucristo. [holy]

Santísimo Sacramento pan que ha sido consagrado por el sacerdote en la Misa. Se guarda en el sagrario para su adoración y para ser llevado a los enfermos. [Blessed Sacrament]

santo persona virtuosa y ejemplar que ha muerto en unión con Dios. Además, la Iglesia ha declarado que esta persona está con Dios en el cielo ahora y para siempre. [saint]

Semana Santa celebración de los sucesos relacionados a la pasión, muerte, y resurrección de Jesús, y el don de la Eucaristía. Se inicia con la conmemoración de la entrada triunfal de Jesús a Jerusalén el Domingo de Ramos; sigue con la conmemoración del regalo que hace de sí mismo en la Eucaristía el Jueves Santo, su muerte el Viernes Santo y su resurrección durante la Vigilia Pascual el Sábado de Gloria. [Holy Week]

Sermón de la Montaña palabras de Jesús que figuran en los capítulos 5 a 7 del Evangelio de San Mateo, en las que Jesús revela cómo Él ha dado plenitud a la ley de Dios entregada a Moisés. El Sermón de la Montaña comienza con las ocho Bienaventuranzas e incluye la oración del Padrenuestro. [Sermon on the Mount]

soberbia imagen falsa de lo que somos que exagera lo que nos corresponde como seres creados por Dios. La soberbia nos pone en competencia con Dios y es uno de los siete pecados capitales. [pride]

T

templanza virtud cardinal moral que nos ayuda a controlar nuestra atracción al placer de manera que nuestros deseos naturales se mantengan dentro de sus límites apropiados. Esta virtud nos ayuda a optar por usar con moderación los bienes creados. [temperance]

tentación atracción, que viene de fuera o de dentro de nosotros mismos, que puede llevarnos a no seguir los mandamientos de Dios [temptation]

testimonio el transmitir a los demás, mediante nuestras palabras y acciones, la fe que se nos ha dado. Cada cristiano tiene el deber de dar testimonio de la buena nueva de Jesucristo que ha llegado a conocer. [witness]

Torá palabra hebrea que significa "instrucción" o "ley". Es también el nombre de los cinco primeros libros del Antiguo Testamento: Génesis, Éxodo, Levítico, Números, y Deuteronomio. [Torah]

Trinidad misterio de la existencia de un Dios en tres personas: Padre, Hijo, y Espíritu Santo [Trinity]

U

Última Cena última comida que cenaron Jesús y sus discípulos la noche antes de que muriera. En la Última Cena, Jesús tomó pan y vino, los bendijo, y dijo que eran su Cuerpo y su Sangre. Cada Misa es un recordatorio de esa última cena. [Last Supper]

una uno de los cuatro calificados de la Iglesia. La Iglesia es una debido a su origen en un Dios único y a su fundador Jesucristo. Jesús, mediante su muerte en la cruz, unió todo a Dios en un cuerpo. Dentro de la unidad de la Iglesia, hay una gran diversidad debido a la riqueza de los dones dados a sus miembros. [one]

unción de los enfermos uno de los siete sacramentos. En este sacramento, la persona enferma es ungida con óleo santo y recibe la fuerza, paz, y coraje para superar las dificultades que trae la enfermedad. [Anointing of the Sick]

V

viático Eucaristía que recibe el moribundo. Es el alimento espiritual para el viaje final que hacemos como cristianos: el viaje a través de la muerte hacia la vida eterna. [viaticum]

Vicario de Cristo título dado al Papa, quien como sucesor de San Pedro, tiene la autoridad de actuar en representación de Cristo. Un vicario es alguien que está o actúa por ella. [Vicar of Christ]

virtud actitud o forma de actuar que nos ayuda a hacer el bien [virtue]

virtudes teologales aquellas virtudes que nos fueron dadas por Dios y no alcanzadas por esfuerzo humano. Ellas son: fe, esperanza, y caridad. [Theological Virtues]

Visitación visita de María a Isabel para contarle la buena nueva de que habrá de ser la madre de Jesús. El saludo de Isabel forma parte del Avemaría. Durante esta visita, María hace su oración de alabanza a Dios: el Magníficat. [Visitation]

vocación llamado que se nos hace en la vida para que seamos las personas que Dios quiere que seamos. También es la forma en que servimos a la Iglesia y al Reino de Dios. Podemos ejercer nuestra vocación como laicos, como miembros de una comunidad religiosa, o como miembros del clero. [vocation]

Acknowledgments

Excerpts from the English translation of *The Roman Missal* © 1973, International Commission on English in the Liturgy, Inc. (ICEL); excerpts from the English translation of *Rite of Penance* © 1974, ICEL; excerpts from the English translation of *A Book of Prayers* © 1982, ICEL; excerpts from the English translation of *Book of Blessings* © 1988, ICEL. All rights reserved. Used with permission.

Excerpts from *The New American Bible with Revised New Testament and Psalms* Copyright © 1991, 1986, 1970 Confraternity of Christian Doctrine, Inc., Washington, DC. Used with permission. All rights reserved. No portion of the *New American Bible* may be reprinted without permission in writing from the copyright holder.

114 Excerpts from Vatican conciliar, postconciliar, and papal documents are from the official translations, Libreria Editrice Vaticana, 00120 Citta del Vaticano.

Illustration

Amanda Hall: 41, 42, 60, 61, 100, 101, 124, 125, 134–135, 172, 174–175, 211, 220
Doron Ben Ami: 254–255
Vitali Konstantinov: 201
David LaFleur: 266, 267, 270, 272–273, 274
Monica Liu: 236–237
Gianna Marino: 68, 162
Hugh Musick: 46, 47, 198, 238
John Stevens: 164
Kristina Swarner: 63, 87, 88, 206, 226, 280
Fred Willingham: 12, 15, 20, 31, 33, 46, 47, 54, 68, 102, 116, 117, 118, 126, 132, 133, 142, 198, 250
Olwyn Whelan: 30

Photography

Unless otherwise acknowledged, photographs are the property of Loyola Press. Page positions are abbreviated as follows: (t) top, (m) middle, (b) bottom, (l) left, (r) right, (l-r) left to right, (bkgr) background, (ins) inset, (cl) clockwise from top right, (all) all images on page.

UNIT 1: 1 From *The Spiritual Journey of St. Ignatius Loyola* by Dora Nikolova Bittau. Photo by Ken Wagner © 1998 Seattle University. **2** (t,l) From *The Spiritual Journey of St. Ignatius Loyola* by Dora Nikolova Bittau. Photo by Ken Wagner © 1998 Seattle University; (bkgr) © Nik Wheeler/CORBIS. **3** (collage) © James Porto/Getty Images/photodisc/Getty Images. **4** (t,l) photodisc/Getty Images; (m,l) © Paul Avis/Getty Images; (b,l) photodisc/Getty Images; (r) photodisc/Getty Images. **5** (all) photodisc/Getty Images. **6** (l-r) © Bill Wittman; photodisc/Getty Images; © Regine M./Getty Images; photodisc/Getty Images. **8** © Jade Albert/Getty Images. **9** © Peter Cade/Getty Images. **10** (t,l) © Diane Meyer; (m) © Hot Ideas/Index Stock; (b,l) photodisc/Getty Images; (b,r) © Howard Sokol/Index Stock. **13** © The Crosiers/Gene Plaisted OSC. **14** (all) Wallraf-Richartz Museum, Cologne. **16** photodisc/Getty Images. **17** © Tony Freeman/PhotoEdit. **18** (l) © Tony Freeman/PhotoEdit; (t,r) photodisc/Getty Images; (b,r) Graphic Used With Permission of Catholic Relief Services. **19** © Steve Satushek/Getty Images. **20** (b) Graphische Sammlung Albertina, Vienna, Austria/The Bridgeman Art Library. **21** © The Crosiers/Gene Plaisted OSC. **22** (b,r) photodisc/Getty Images. **23** (t) © Myrleen F. Cate/PhotoEdit; (b) © Stephen Simpson/Getty Images. **24** © The Crosiers/Gene Plaisted OSC. **25** © David Young-Wolff/PhotoEdit. **26** (t,l) © Michael Newman/PhotoEdit; (b,r) photodisc/Getty Images. **27** © Harry Sieplinga, HMS Images/Getty Images. **28** photodisc/Getty Images. **29** (t,l) photodisc/Getty Images; (b,l) photodisc/Getty Images; (r) © Alexander Walter/Getty Images. **32** (ins) © 2004, David Wakely Photography; (bkgr) DiAMAR. **34** (t) © Scala/Art Resource, NY; (m) © David Young-Wolff/PhotoEdit; (b,l) © Peter Cade/Getty Images; (b,r) © Myrleen F. Cate/PhotoEdit. **35** (t,l) © Inc. Bokelberg G&J Images/Getty Images; (b) photodisc/Getty Images. **36** (cl) © Alexandra Michaels/Getty Images; © Steve Satushek/Getty Images; photodisc/Getty Images; photodisc/Getty Images; photodisc/Getty Images. **37** (all) photodisc/Getty Images. **38** (bkgr) © The Crosiers/Gene Plaisted OSC. **39** (bkgr) © The Crosiers/Gene Plaisted OSC. **40** © Daniel Pangbourne Media/Getty Images.

UNIT 2: 45 (t,r) © Archivo Iconografico, S.A./CORBIS. **48** (ins) © David Seed Photography/Getty Images. **49** © Johner/Photonica. **50** (t,l) Jeanette Kuvin Orin; (m) © David Woods/CORBIS; (b,l) © Myrleen F. Cate/PhotoEdit; (b,r) photodisc/Getty Images. **51** © Marks Productions/Getty Images. **52** Courtesy of Riverside Church, New York, NY. **55** photodisc/Getty Images. **56** © Tomonari Tsuji/Photonica. **57** © Don Smetzer/Getty Images. **58** (l) © Journal Courier/Steve Warmowski/The Image Works; (t,r) Courtesy of Riverside Church, New York, NY; (m,r) Used With Permission of Catholic Charities USA; (b,r) © Jon Feingersh/CORBIS. **59** © Arthur Tilley/Getty Images. **62** © David Lees/CORBIS. **64** Courtesy of David Huasacca Condori, Peru; (bkgr) © Phil Martin Photography. **66** (t,l) photodisc/Getty Images; (b,l) photodisc/Getty Images; (t,r) © Jose Luis Pelaez, Inc./CORBIS; (b,r) © Meltem Aktas/Imago inc. **67** (l) © Frank Herholdt/Getty Images; (t,r) © David Roth/Getty Images; (b,r) © Robin Davies/Getty Images. **68** (t) © The J. Paul Getty Museum. **69** Written by Nana Quparadze, a Georgian iconographer. Reprinted by Permission of the Holy Resurrection Orthodox Church, Singapore (Orthodox Metrolitinate of Hong Kong & SE Asia). **70** (l) © Solomon Raj; (butterflies) photodisc/Getty Images. **71** (t,l) © Sean Justice/Getty Images; (b,l) © Joe Polillio/Getty Images; (butterflies) photodisc/Getty Images. **72** (ins) Museo di San Marco dell' Angelico, Florence, Italy/The Bridgeman Art Library; (bkgr) © G Ryan & S Beyer/Getty Images. **73** © Marc Grimberg/Getty Images. **74** (t,l) photodisc/Getty Images; (b,l) photodisc/Getty Images; (t,r) Written by Nana Quparadze, a Georgian iconographer. Reprinted by Permission of the Holy Resurrection Orthodox Church, Singapore (Orthodox Metrolitanate of Hong Kong & S E Asia). **75** © Todd Davidson/Getty Images. **76** (l-r) photodisc/Getty Images; photodisc/Getty Images; © Davies & Starr/Getty Images. **77** (t,l) photodisc/Getty Images; (m,r) photodisc/Getty Images; (b,l) © Chris Simpson/Getty Images. **79** photodisc/Getty Images. **80** © Walter Hodges/CORBIS.

UNIT 3: 81 Courtesy of the Archives of the Sisters of the Blessed Sacrament, Bensalem, PA. **82** (t,l) Courtesy of the Archives of the Sisters of the Blessed Sacrament, Bensalem, PA; (all ins) Courtesy of the Archives of the Sisters of the Blessed Sacrament, Bensalem, PA; (bkgr) photodisc/Getty Images. **83** © Kendall McMinimy/Getty Images. **84** © Scala/Art Resource, NY. **85** (l-r) © Robert Brenner/PhotoEdit; © Erlanson Productions/Getty Images; © David Young-Wolff/PhotoEdit. **86** (l) © Werner Bokelberg/Getty Images; (r) © Bob Borton. **89** photodisc/Getty Images. **90** (t,l) © Steve/Mary Skjold/Index Stock; (b,l) photodisc/Getty Images; (t,r) © Robert Lentz. Reproductions Available from Bridge Building Images, www.bridge building.com; (b,r) Courtesy of the Archives of the Sisters of the Blessed Sacrament, Bensalem, PA. **92** Courtesy of Immaculate Conception Church, Earlington, KY/Photo by Ray Giardinella. **93** (l-r) © AFP/CORBIS; © John H. White; © Bettmann/CORBIS. **94** (l) © Bettmann/CORBIS. **95** © 2004, David Wakely Photography. **96** © 2004, David Wakely Photography. **98** (t,l) © Scala/Art Resource, NY; (b,l) © Andrea Jemolo/CORBIS; (r) photodisc/Getty Images; (b,r) photodisc/Getty Images. **99** (cl) photodisc/Getty Images; photodisc/Getty Images; (t,l) © Chip Simons/Getty Images. **102** (t,r) © Phil McCarten/PhotoEdit. **104** photodisc/Getty Images. **105** © Denis Boissavy/Getty Images. **106** (l) © Royalty Free/CORBIS; (t,r) © He Qi, www.heqiarts.com; (m,r) photodisc/Getty Images; (b,r) © Myrleen F. Cate/PhotoEdit. **107** © Arthur Tilley/Getty Images. **108** © ARS, NY, 1913. © Réunion des Musées Nationaux/Art Resource, NY. **109** © 2002 Benaki Museum Athens. **110** (l) © Jim Cummins/Getty Images; (b) © Bill Wittman. **112** © Scala/Art Resource, NY. **113** © Michael Krasowitz/Getty Images. **114** (t,l) © Tony Freeman/PhotoEdit; (b,l) photodisc/Getty Images; (t,r) Peter Willi/Private Collection/The Bridgeman Art Library; (b,r) © Jeff Greenberg/Index Stock. **115** (cl) SW Productions; © Myrleen F. Cate/PhotoEdit; © The Crosiers/Gene Plaisted OSC. **116** © The Crosiers/Gene Plaisted OSC. **118** (t,l) Creatas. **119** © Steve Raymer/CORBIS.

UNIT 4: 121 Mary Evans Picture Library. **122** (t) Mary Evans Picture Library; (ins) David Atkinson; (bkgr) Hermitage, St. Petersburg, Russia/The Bridgeman Art Library. **124** (t) Cliché Bibliothèque Nationale de France,